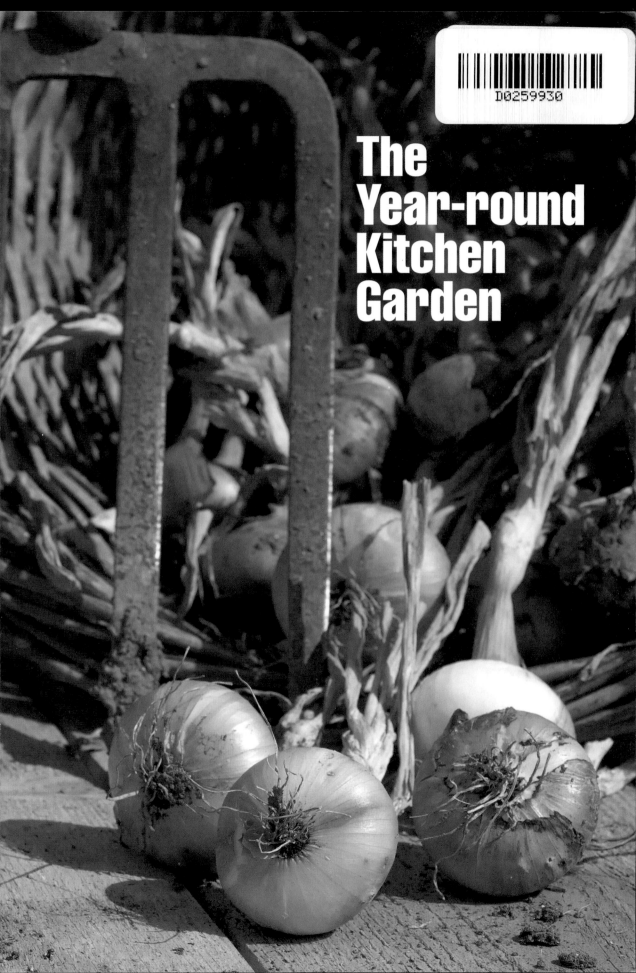

The Year-round Kitchen Garden

Published by
The Reader's Digest Association Limited
London ■ New York ■ Sydney ■ Montreal

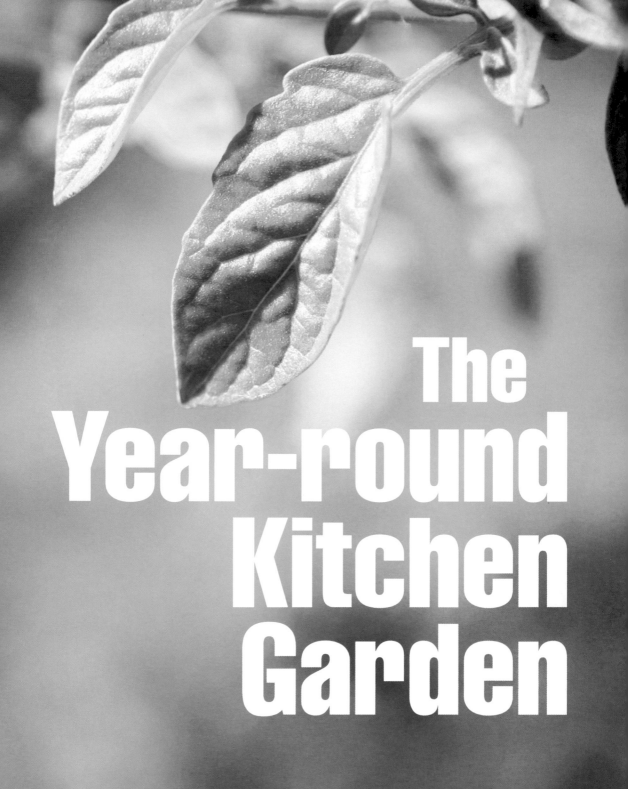

The Year-round Kitchen Garden

Expert advice on growing food in your garden through the seasons

Contents

Winter

Autumn

Introduction

There are few things more satisfying than growing your own food and the kitchen garden can provide you and your family with a supply of tasty and healthy crops all year round. Whether it's vegetables, herbs or fruit, there will be something in season, whatever the weather.

In Britain we are blessed with a temperate climate which allows us to grow a wide variety of different plants. But we are also governed by the seasons which determine just when these plants will thrive. Few plants are productive all year – and fruit, vegetables and herbs are no exception – but with careful planning, the kitchen garden can provide crops throughout the year.

Timing is the key to success: if you sow your seeds at the right moment you'll get a better yield when the plants are ready to harvest; stagger your plantings correctly, and you'll ensure a continuous supply of crops. You also need to maintain the kitchen garden – whether it's weeding, watering or mulching, for example – and there are certain jobs that need to be done at certain times. Follow the simple guidelines here and you can enjoy a happy and fruitful gardening year.

This book is organised into four chapters, one for each season. Each chapter is further divided into sections on vegetables, herbs and fruit, which detail the most important tasks to be done in each season. In this book, spring is taken as being March to May, summer is June to August, autumn is September to November and winter is December to February. However, the seasons will vary depending on where you live and you should be guided by local weather conditions when making decisions about what jobs need doing and when.

Spring

The vegetable garden

Although there is no real end to the cropping year in a well-planned kitchen garden, the onset of spring feels like the beginning of a new year. As the long days of winter draw to an end and the weather warms up, conditions in the garden improve enough to begin planting out for the season ahead.

Spring checklist

■ **Continue preparing seedbeds** for new plantings. Break the soil down to a roughly level surface, so that it can dry out during sunny or windy weather. This will help you to create a fine surface, or tilth, when the seedbed is raked level.

■ **Monitor soil temperature** to see how quickly it is warming up. The seeds of many vegetables need temperatures of 5–7°C (40–45°F) in the upper layer of soil before they will germinate.

■ **Warm the soil** before sowing or planting by covering areas with cloches, low polythene tunnels or black plastic sheeting. If the weather is dry and windy, remove the covers to allow the soil to dry before sowing.

■ **Prepare trenches** for planting runner beans, peas, marrows or pumpkins in late spring or early summer (see page 12).

■ **Dig areas as they become clear** of crops and compost the plant waste. Dig in any overwintering green manures.

■ **If the soil is wet**, dig trenches 15–20cm (6–8in) deep and wide at 1.2m (4ft) intervals. This creates mini raised beds in between, with improved drainage.

■ **Order seeds** and young vegetable plants for delivery later. Although young plants and seedlings are becoming available now, do not be tempted to buy too early in cold areas unless you can provide them with the protection they may need.

■ **Make early sowings** of crops such as beetroot, broad beans, carrot, lettuce, peas, radish,

To test the soil temperature, insert an outdoor thermometer into the upper 8–10cm (3–4in) layer of earth and leave it for about an hour.

spinach and turnips when soil conditions become suitable. Choose early varieties of these crops where possible.

■ **Sow many of the cabbage** family outdoors, including cauliflowers, kale, kohl rabi and sprouting broccoli, all of which mature much later in the year. Choose different varieties to give a continuity of supply: cauliflowers, for example, can be autumn-maturing (early to late autumn), winter-maturing (late winter through to early spring) and spring-maturing (early spring until early summer the next year).

■ **Plant out bulb onions** and onion sets.

■ **Plant early potatoes** in March and maincrop potatoes towards the end of April.

■ **Plant asparagus** and globe artichokes.

■ **Sow root vegetables** outdoors. Dig down two spade depths to allow deeper root penetration and better quality vegetables.

■ **Sow hardier vegetables** outdoors when the soil reaches a minimum temperature of 7–7.5°C (44–45°F).

■ **Begin successional sowings** of quick-maturing crops such as lettuce and radish, and crops that you don't want maturing all at once, such as peas and dwarf beans.

■ **Sow runner beans**, which like a warmed soil, later rather than earlier, in double rows. Position supports as soon as the seedlings emerge, as bean seedlings grow rapidly.

■ **Inspect any vegetables** that you have stored over winter at regular intervals. Remove any showing signs of mould or rot before they infect their neighbours. Use up quickly those that show signs of growth or withering. Stored crops could include beetroot, carrots, garlic, onions, potatoes, shallots, swedes and turnips.

■ **Plant out autumn** and winter-maturing brussels sprouts.

■ **Begin to harden off** and plant out hardy crops, such as peas, started off in pots under glass in winter.

■ **Mulch perennial crops**, such as rhubarb or artichokes, with well-rotted organic matter. This will help suppress weeds and retain moisture.

■ **Protect seedbeds** and seedlings from birds by covering them with fleece or netting, or using bird scarers. Brassicas are particularly vulnerable, and wood pigeons will feed on any cauliflowers they can reach.

■ **During dry periods**, take the opportunity to hoe off weed seedlings, but remember that disturbing the soil encourages more weed seeds to germinate as the weather turns milder.

■ **Water young plants regularly** to ensure they keep growing steadily.

■ **Look out for signs** of potential pests, such as slug damage or aphid infestation. Pests are more easily dealt with if spotted early.

■ **Protect the cabbage family** from flea beetle and cabbage root fly damage by covering with fleece or fitting 'collars' round individual plants.

■ **Harvest asparagus shoots** in established beds, once they are about 15cm (6in) high. Slice the stem 2–3cm (1in) below soil level.

■ **Continue harvesting** the flowering shoots of sprouting broccoli varieties so that more are produced.

■ **Start a long-term planting** of asparagus (it takes five years to produce spears). Set the crowns in trenches 10cm (4in) deep, 30cm (12in) apart, with 45cm (18in) between the crowns.

Vegetable seeds come in a wide and colourful array of shapes and sizes; spring is the time for sowing many different varieties, both indoors and out.

Preparing a planting trench

Mark out a trench and dig out a section at one end; half fill with kitchen and garden waste. Dig out the next section and put this soil on top of the waste. Continue until the trench has been filled, covering the last section with the soil from the first. Leave for about a month or two for the waste to compost down.

Trench composting

You can provide a source of nourishment and moisture for tall peas, runner beans, marrows, squash and pumpkins by composting a supply of waste in a trench. Mark out a trench 30cm (12in) wide and dig it out to the depth of a spade blade. Fill to half its depth with kitchen and garden waste and cover with soil (see left). Leave to settle for a month or two. For pumpkins or beans on 'wigwams', dig a pit 1m (3ft) wide for each plant and fill the same way.

Avoiding later pest problems

Pests and diseases become more prevalent as the weather turns milder. Slugs start to feed soon after hatching, but if this first generation can be controlled it will be months before the population builds up.

■ **Look for aphids** on the outer leaves of cabbages, cauliflowers and other vegetables.
■ **Help control blackfly** on broad beans by pinching out the growing tips when they begin to flower.

Protecting seedlings from slugs

The juicy young leaves of seedlings will always attract slugs but there are various ways to deter them.

Place a flower pot over the seedling and scatter grit around the rim; the pot acts as a guide and keeps grit off the plant.

Cut a collar from a plastic bottle using pinking shears; slugs and snails will not climb over the serrated edge.

Place the base of a clear plastic bottle filled with old beer near young plants, to act as a trap – or use upturned grapefruit skins.

Sowing and planting

Early spring is the time for putting into practice the plans you made during the winter months, and for sowing and planting those crops that you enjoy eating. The weather and your garden conditions will play an important part in the precise timing of your sowing and planting, as will the varieties you choose.

Varieties

If you look through seed catalogues or along a stand of seed packets in the garden centre, you will see that some crops, such as peas, carrots and potatoes, have early and maincrop varieties. Maincrops are sown later in the season than earlies, and usually take longer to mature. You can sow some early varieties of carrot in late summer, as they are quick to mature, but with lettuce it is vital to sow the right variety for the season.

Timing

Many crops can be sown or planted over several months. Bear in mind that most seeds and young plants can only grow when the soil temperature reaches a minimum requirement; the danger of sowing too early is not frost, but that seeds will sit in cold, damp soil and rot before they germinate.

Many of the earlier sowings will be more successful if made under glass – a greenhouse or coldframe – or with cloche protection than in open ground. Sowings made under glass in modular trays incur less root disturbance than those made in trays or pots and then pricked out. This is a useful way of getting a head start and avoiding the unpredictability of the weather at the start of the year. Using modular trays is also a way to minimise root disturbance when transplanting vegetables, as they are planted with an intact rootball, avoiding the risk of tearing young roots as you tease seedlings apart.

Cover young seedlings with cloches. This will help protect them from both cold and damage by pests.

Spacing crops

Plants grow better without too much competition, which is why regular weeding and correct spacing are important. It is worth thinning seedlings in stages rather than all in one go, to avoid gaps, conserve moisture and suppress weeds. Later thinnings can often be used in salads, or as immature or baby vegetables, leaving the rest wider-spaced to mature fully. You may in any case prefer smaller roots and cabbages, in which case grow them closer together; the seed packet usually states whether the variety is suitable for growing in this way.

Extended harvesting

For the harvesting period to last as long as possible, make a number of small successional sowings every few weeks and include early, maincrop and

Seeds large and small

Space large seeds, such as peas and beans, individually at regular intervals in a tray, or sow two or three seeds in small pots and press them down into the compost.

Tiny seeds are more difficult to sow. Mix them thoroughly with some dry silver sand and sprinkle this over the surface of a pot of compost to distribute evenly.

seasonal varieties. Protecting early and late crops with cloches is another way to extend the harvest. With peas and beans, regular picking in itself prolongs the season.

The yield you can expect from a crop is greatly influenced by the conditions in which it grows. If your soil is well prepared, regularly enriched with organic matter and kept weed free, your yield will be much higher than where the soil is dry, weedy and exhausted of nutrients. Other influencing factors are the weather and your choice of variety; some varieties simply yield more heavily than others.

Crops in spring

Spring is the best time for sowing seeds under cover and for planting out many crops, including perennial asparagus and both globe and jerusalem artichokes.

Peas and beans
Sow early varieties of peas in 8–10cm (3–4in) pots, two or three seeds per pot, then place in a cool greenhouse or coldframe, if not already done in late winter. The plants will be large enough for planting out by mid-spring. Plant them 8–10cm (3–4in) apart, preferably in warm soil to avoid any check to growth.

Alternatively, fill a length of plastic guttering with seed compost and sow the seeds in that. Leave in the greenhouse or coldframe until mid to late spring. Then dig a shallow trench outdoors and simply slide

Successional planting

Many vegetables grow quickly and mature all at once, so sowing little and often – a technique known as successional sowing – is the best way to maintain a regular supply.

- **Peas, spinach, spinach beet and dwarf beans (also known as french, string or kidney beans)** Make successional sowings of these crops every three weeks. Sow beans in double rows.
- **Lettuces and radishes** Sow every two to three weeks. Sow between rows of slow growers, such as parsnips, for efficient use of space; this is known as intercropping.
- **Salad onions** Sow every three to four weeks, thinly in 7–8cm (3in) wide bands, to avoid the need for thinning.

Pinch out the tops of broad beans once in full flower; this will help with the control of blackfly.

the row of peas into that. This technique gets plants off to a good start in cold areas and makes transplantation easier.

■ **As the weather warms,** remove cloches from autumn-sown peas, but harden them off first by removing alternate cloches during the day and ventilating them increasingly at night for a couple of weeks.

■ **Thin peas sown in autumn** or late winter by removing alternate plants.

■ **Sow early peas** and broad beans outdoors as a follow-on crop to those raised in pots, or sown outdoors under cloches or in polythene tunnels.

■ **Harden off and plant out** broad beans sown in pots under cover in winter, 25–30cm (10–12in) apart.

Cabbage family Sow brussels sprouts, sprouting broccoli and varieties of summer cabbage and cauliflower in pots or in a seedbed for transplanting in May or June.

■ **Transplant autumn-sown** spring cabbages early, spacing plants about 30cm (12in) apart.

■ **Finish harvesting** last year's brussels sprouts as the last 'buttons' swell; snap off the leafy tops and use as greens. Harvest winter cabbages, cutting the whole head,

and start picking the secondary crop of leafy greens produced by the stumps of previously harvested cabbages.

■ **Harvest spring greens** planted in autumn. Pick some of the young leaves, as more will develop, or remove alternate plants so that those left form a head.

■ **Harvest kale by picking** the young shoots, leaving the large outer leaves intact to fuel the plants' growth.

Onion family Onions and shallots can be started off from seed under glass or planted out as sets ('mini' bulbs). Outdoors, they need a sunny position in fertile, cultivated ground. It is a race against time to get enough growth on the plant before the bulbs start to swell after midsummer's day. Hand-weed carefully to avoid disturbing their shallow roots. Check them regularly until they have started to root, as birds foraging for food often move them about. Replant them if necessary.

Straight sowing

One way to mark a straight drill in a seed bed is to press the handle of a rake or hoe into the soil to make a groove.

■ **Sow the seed of bulb onions** and shallots in modular trays or pots under glass.

■ **Sow leeks in modular trays** or pots in the greenhouse. Sow four or five seeds per pot to transplant in late spring. Lift mature leeks as required. If you need the ground for planting other crops in April, lift any that remain and heel them in spare ground out of the sun.

■ **Sow the seed of salad onions** from late March in short rows.

■ **Inspect stored onions and garlic** and dispose of any showing signs of rot or mould. Use up any that are shooting.

■ **Plant out onion sets** in late spring, 15cm (6in) apart, with 15cm (6in) between rows, and 1cm (1/2in) deep to give medium-sized, nicely rounded bulbs. If possible, select smaller sets as they are less likely to 'bolt'. 'Golden Ball' is a good cultivar that tolerates later planting.

■ **Transplant shallots** sown earlier so that only the tips protrude, spacing them 15cm (6in) apart in rows 20cm (8in) apart.

Chitting potatoes

Early potatoes are chitted in late winter or early spring; maincrops are chitted two to three weeks later. Lay them in seed trays or egg trays, rose end up (the end with most buds, or 'eyes'), in a cool, light frost-free place. About six weeks later each potato will have formed four to five shoots 2–3cm (1in) long. When conditions are suitable, plant out the tubers.

■ **Transplant bulb onions** sown earlier in spring, burying them just below the soil surface. A spacing of 25–30cm (10–12in) apart and 25–30cm (10–12in) between the rows is ideal. The bulbs must be kept well-watered until they have established.

Potatoes For a greater chance of a successful crop, it is advisable to buy seed potatoes that are certified disease-free, rather than be tempted to plant tubers you have bought from the greengrocer or supermarket. The size of seed potatoes depends on the variety, but they should be about the size of a hen's egg.

There are two main types of potato: earlies and maincrop. Earlies are planted in early spring and need only 14–15 weeks in the ground to produce tender 'new' potatoes for immediate use. These are the potatoes to grow in a small garden because they take up less space and are in the ground for a shorter time. Maincrop potatoes have a longer growing season (about 20 weeks) and need more space, but they produce heavier yields, which also store well.

Before planting, you need to sprout, or chit, potatoes indoors (see left). Earlies are chitted in late winter or very early in spring, for planting out in March or early April. Maincrop varieties are chitted two to three weeks later for planting in late spring.

Soil temperature at the planting depth should be at least 6°C (43°F) for four or five days before planting, so that the shoots will grow unchecked. Potatoes like a soil that is fertile but not too rich, otherwise leaf growth is encouraged at the expense of roots. The storage life of the roots will also be reduced.

■ **Plant earlies in March** and earth up to protect new shoots from potential late frosts. Once the threat of frost has passed, continue to earth up when the tops (haulms) of early potatoes are about 25cm (10in) high. Draw up the soil to cover the bottom 12–13cm (5in) of the stems so that tubers form on the buried sideshoots.

Sowing seeds in modular trays helps get vegetables, like celeriac, off to a good start before planting out.

■ **Plant maincrop potatoes** in late spring. Space them 40cm (16in) apart with 75cm (2ft 6in) between rows. Grow them apart from other crops, if possible; their abundant leafy growth takes up a lot of space above ground as well as below.

Root crops Make the first sowings of early varieties of beetroot, carrot and turnip in early spring, unless the soil is cold and wet, in which case wait for it to warm up. For the earliest sowings, use cloches, or cover the soil for a week or two with plastic sheeting to provide warmer conditions and encourage rapid seed germination.

Many root crops that mature well into the second half of the year can be sown outdoors in late spring: beetroot, carrot, parsnip, swede and turnip. The timing of sowing is a bit of a balancing act: beetroot, for example, if sown too early, may 'bolt', producing premature seed.

■ **Sow parsnips outdoors** in late March or April in rows or in blocks 10cm (4in) apart with 10cm (4in) between rows, to prevent the roots from becoming too large and misshapen; the longer the growing season, the larger the parsnips grow. Do not grow close to carrots as they both attract carrot root fly. As parsnips are slow to germinate, sow radish or beetroot in between as markers; these fast-maturing crops will be ready for pulling before the parsnip roots start to develop.

■ **Sow beetroot seeds** 15cm (6in) apart with 15cm (6in) between rows, to grow medium-sized, nicely rounded beets.

■ **Sow the seed of celeriac** under cover in modular trays.

■ **Sow maincrop carrots** in shallow seed drills, only 1cm (½in) deep. Sow thinly, 5cm (2in) apart in rows 15cm (6in) apart, to reduce the need for thinning out and reduce risk of carrot root fly. Water the drills immediately after sowing if the soil is dry; do not overwater, as the plants would then produce too much leaf and the roots would split, especially if watered heavily after a period of dry weather.

TIP Cover carrots with fleece tucked into the soil to give an earlier crop and to protect against carrot fly.

Sow the seed for maincrop carrots thinly in shallow drills and water well afterwards.

Perennial crops Globe artichokes and asparagus, in particular, need a lot of space and should be planted in a sheltered, sunny position. The soil should be well drained, deeply dug, enriched with plenty of rotted manure or garden compost and cleared of all traces of perennial weeds. These long-term crops need two years to establish before you can enjoy a harvest.

■ **Cut offsets of globe artichokes** from the edge of established plants and set them just deep enough to stand upright, about 5cm (2in), and 50cm (20in) apart. Alternatively, buy and plant small specimens. Cover with fleece if frost threatens.

■ **Plant asparagus crowns** as soon as possible to prevent them drying out. Dig a trench 45cm (18in) deep and incorporate plenty of well-rotted organic matter. Scrape up the soil at the bottom of the trench to form a slight ridge. Place the crowns in the trench, spreading out the roots on either side of the ridge. Space crowns 30cm (12in) apart and rows 45cm (18in) apart. Fill the trench and fork in more compost.

Harvest the asparagus spears when they about 15cm (6in) tall. Cook soon after picking to enjoy the best flavour.

■ **Start to harvest** established asparagus plants when spears are 15cm (6in) tall.

■ **Plant jerusalem artichoke** tubers 30cm (12in) apart and 10cm (4in) deep in well-prepared soil; they will tolerate light shade. The plants grow tall, reaching 3m (10ft), and will crop this year.

Salad crops Continue to protect early sowings with cloches or polythene tunnels, giving ventilation on sunny days. Thin when necessary; there may be pickings in a mild season. Make successional sowings of lettuce, radish and spinach in open ground, preferably warmed by plastic sheeting.

Tender crops If you wait for the soil to warm up before sowing tender crops, they will just produce leafy growth and little or no crop, so they must be started off under protection. Most also hate root disturbance, so sow them in individual small pots. Plants that start growing indoors must have two to three weeks of hardening off before being transplanted into the garden soil. If you buy your young plants from a garden centre or nursery, they should have already been hardened off, but it is worth checking.

■ **Move aubergines, peppers** and tomatoes outside to grow successfully when the soil temperature reaches 10°C (50°F).

■ **Courgettes, marrows and squashes** can all be grown outside, but generally tend to do better in a coldframe or polythene tunnel. They prefer high humidity and may suffer from mildew if grown outside in dry conditions. Transplant them with minimum root disturbance, as even slight damage to the roots can result in the roots rotting and, eventually, in the loss of the plant.

■ **Young sweetcorn plants** should be about 15–20cm (6–8in) high before they are planted out. Transplant them in their moist peat pots into square or rectangular blocks (as they are pollinated by wind), with the plants spaced 35cm (14in) apart, with 35cm (14in) between rows.

When spring arrives there is a rapid revival in growth so it's time to tidy perennial herbs and start the propagation of new plants. Sow tender herbs under glass and hardy ones outside and in pots. By late spring you'll be gathering the first fragrant tips.

Spring checklist

■ **Order the seeds of annual herbs** before the main sowing season, or get ahead by buying seedlings.

■ **Tidy herbs in beds and borders** before new growth gets under way. Clear the dead foliage of herbaceous herbs, such as salad burnet and fennel, then weed and prick over the soil with a fork.

■ **Feed perennial herbs** such as marjoram and tarragon with bone meal or a high-potash granular fertiliser.

■ **Warm the ground** before sowing by covering prepared soil with cloches, plastic sheeting or low polythene tunnels. Start sowing two to three weeks later.

■ **Prune lavender, sage and rosemary** in a mild season; avoid cutting back into old wood, which may not regenerate. Cut out any damaged, straggly or misplaced shoots.

■ **Plant out potted hardy herbs** used indoors over winter after feeding with general fertiliser and hardening them off for 10–14 days. Keep tender herbs frost free in a coldframe or greenhouse until late spring.

■ **Thin early sowings** of salad and other annual herbs to 10cm (4in) apart, then water to settle the disturbed seedlings.

■ **Thin out the seedlings** of those herbs sown under glass in autumn.

■ **Pot up strong seedlings** in 10cm (4in) pots for planting in containers or standing on the kitchen windowsill.

■ **Top-dress herbs** in large containers by replacing the top 2–5cm (1–2in) of soil with fresh potting compost.

■ **Take root cuttings** of mint, bergamot, chamomile, hyssop, sweet cicely, sweet woodruff and tarragon.

■ **Check any layers** taken the previous year. Pot them up if they have rooted.

Plant up a pot with your favourite herbs and create a mini herb garden that's perfect on the patio (see page 20).

■ **Harden off cuttings** rooted and potted up in late summer last year under glass, and plant out in permanent positions.

■ **Take soft-tip cuttings** from the new shoots of sage and tarragon.

■ **Support tall herbs,** such as angelica or fennel before they are damaged by winds.

■ **Crumble dried herbs** from last season and scatter them over newly sown flower and vegetable seeds to confuse soil pests.

■ **Divide perennial clump-forming** herbs, but keep transplants watered in dry weather.

■ **Sow essential herbs** such as basil and parsley under glass.

■ **Sow short-lived annual herbs** such as chervil, coriander and dill to provide pickings later in the year. Sow under glass in April and plant out in late May after hardening off.

Planting a herb tower

Herb pots – tall pots with holes around the sides – are ideal for growing a selection of herbs in a small space. They have protruding cups around their sides that support the plants growing there. There is a danger with these kinds of tall pots that the plants at the top will become waterlogged and the ones at the bottom dry out. To make sure that water spreads evenly through the pot, include a central core of grit when you plant.

1 Position a pipe in the centre of the pot. An offcut of plastic plumbing pipe or the cardboard tube from a roll of kitchen towel will do. Hold the pipe steady then fill around it with compost as far as the first holes.

2 Start to introduce plants. Push them through the holes from the inside, firming the compost around them as you go. Work your way up until you reach the top. Put trailing plants in the sides and bushy ones in the top.

3 Before you can plant in the space at the top of the pot, fill the pipe with grit to the level of the compost in the pot.

4 Gently ease the pipe out so that you leave a core of grit behind in the compost, then plant up the top layer of the pot.

Repotting herbs

French lavender (*Lavandula stoechas*), rosemaries such as *Rosmarinus officinalis* 'Prostratus', and lemon verbena can be trimmed to shape now, before potting on or repotting. Cut out dead wood, shorten very long shoots and remove one or two older branches on lemon verbena; lightly clip evergreens to a balanced shape.

■ **Pot on young plants** into the next size pot, using a soil-based compost and putting plenty of drainage material in the bottom.

■ **Repot larger specimens** by carefully knocking them from their pots. Tease the outer 2–3cm (1in) of compost from the roots and replace in the same container, working fresh soil-based compost between the roots with your fingers.

Propagation

Many perennial herbs can be propagated now. This will ensure young, more vigorous replacements for ageing plants.

Dividing herbs You can divide up pots of culinary herbs, such as parsley, coriander and basil, bought from a supermarket.

■ **Stand the pot** in a cool, well-lit place and water if dry. Grandually turn down the plastic sleeve a little day by day. Once the sleeve has been completely removed and the plant does not droop, tap it out of its pot.

■ **Cut the rootball** into segments and pot up in 10cm (4in) pots of soil-based compost. Water and stand in a lightly shaded place to grown on.

To divide perennial herbs, dig up the clumps and split them with a spade or sharp knife, or tear them apart with your fingers. Replant the outer portions in fresh soil, discarding the woody centre.

■ **Divide chives, lemon balm,** marjoram, mint, sorrel and tarragon in early spring.

■ **Late in the season** you can divide any of the above, plus lovage, rue, salad burnet, thyme, winter savory and any herbs growing in cold gardens.

Cuttings You can take soft-tip cuttings of sage and tarragon in late spring.

■ **Trim off the tips of young shoots** and trim so that you have a small piece of healthy stem just below a leaf joint; remove the bottom pair of leaves.

■ **Insert your cuttings** into pots of sharp sand and leave in a mini propagator or on a windowsill out of direct sunlight until they take root.

Some perennial herbs like mint, tarragon and bergamot can be propagated by root cuttings taken early in the season.

■ **Dig up a healthy plant** and look at the roots; pick out some about as thick as a pencil and cut from the plant near the crown.

■ **Cut up each root** into 7–10cm (3–4in) lengths. Make a straight cut at the top and a slanting cut at the bottom of each piece so that you know which end is which.

■ **Insert six to eight cuttings** around the edge of a pot filled with cuttings compost so that the top of each one is level with the soil. Cover with a fine layer of grit and place in a coldframe or sheltered place outdoors.

Layering herbs You can layer several different herbs such as thyme, sage and rosemary.

■ **Gently pull down** a low, strong-growing branch so that it touches the ground at least 8cm (3in) from its tip, scoop out a small hole and fill with moist potting compost.

■ **Peg the stem down** just below the surface with a stone or bent wire, mound more compost over the pegged area and leave until autumn.

■ **Take multiple layers** from old rosemary and other tall woody plants like lavender by pegging down the bare, leggy stems to the ground as described above.

The young shoots of sage can be used as soft-tip cuttings to create new plants and increase your stock of this handy culinary herb.

Dropping This is a similar technique to layering whereby you plant an old woody plant, such as rosemary or lavender, at a deeper level in the soil to encourage roots to develop on the buried stems

■ **Dig up an old plant** with a good sized rootball and excavate the hole 30cm (12in) deeper. Return the plant to the deeper hole.

■ **Refill with soil, mounding it up** around the stems. Leave until autumn.

Herb hedges

Small aromatic evergreens like box, lavender, rosemary and semi-evergreen hyssop have traditionally been used to make low hedges for edging or sheltering herb borders and creating divisions or intricate knots in more formal gardens. Evergreen herbs are best planted in April or in early autumn, when pot-grown plants will establish quickly.

■ **Choose small, bushy plants** as these will settle in faster than the larger specimens. Water them well an hour or two before planting out.

■ **Mark out the position** of the new hedge. Use a garden line or string pulled taut for straight edges; for curves, lay a hosepipe on the ground or sprinkle a trail of sand.

■ **Dig or fork over** a 30cm (12in) wide trench along the line. Break up the excavated soil, and mix in a little bone meal and garden compost to improve the texture.

■ **Knock the plants** from their pots, and plant them about 23–25cm (9–10in) apart along the row, with the top of the rootballs at ground level. Carefully firm the soil around each plant.

■ **Water in the plants** well and then lightly trim the tips of their shoots; this will encourage early branching.

The fruit garden

By spring, stored fruit from last year's crop has been used up but, at the same time, new blossom appears to herald the harvest yet to come. Some blooms, however, are vulnerable to late frosts and need protection if you want to enjoy the fruits of your labour.

Spring checklist

■ **Check fruits in store** frequently as the end of the keeping season approaches, and use up the good samples quickly.

■ **Weed around mature fruit** and lightly cultivate the surface of the surrounding soil with a fork, ready for feeding and mulching.

■ **Protect fruit blossom** from late frost with fleece, if hard frost is forecast. This applies to early peach and nectarine fruitlets as well as other small fruit trees and bushes, and wall-trained apples, pears, plums and cherries in flower.

■ **Protect peaches** and nectarines from peach leaf curl by covering the trees with screens, and by applying a copper-based fungicide spray.

■ **Apply a general or high-potash** fertiliser to bush and cane fruit and trained trees.

■ **Watch for signs of pests and disease,** including scale insects, and make headway by treating at first sight.

■ **Check blackcurrants** for big bud mites; infected buds are conspicuous and are easily removed for destruction.

■ **Remove grease bands** from around fruit trees in April.

■ **Water new fruit plants** in dry weather, especially those near walls and fences where the soil is sheltered from rain. Apply water at a rate of 25 litres per m² (5 gallons per sq yd) a week. Hoe regularly to remove competing weeds.

■ **Inspect supports** for trained fruit, and replace or repair them if necessary. Check and loosen ties before new growth starts. Tie in new stems while they are flexible.

■ **Train and tie in** the new fruiting canes of blackberries, hybrid berries and other brambles, fanning them out in their cropping positions.

■ **Thin spurs** on trained apples and pears; complete this and all winter pruning, except for stone fruits, as soon as possible.

Strawberries that were potted up last autumn and brought into the greenhouse over winter should be beginning to flower and fruit. Brush each flower with a soft paintbrush to transfer pollen between the plants and so encourage fruits to form.

Rhubarb can be forced into early growth by covering with a special pot or simply an old bucket with a hole in the base.

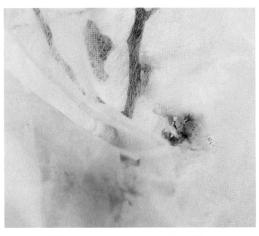

Horticultural fleece can be draped over delicate blooms to offer protection overnight. It's a finely woven, lightweight material that can last for several seasons.

■ **Prune new bush** and cane fruit before growth starts.

■ **Cover rhubarb grown outdoors** with forcing pots, boxes or buckets to produce early tender stalks.

■ **Plant autumn-fruiting** raspberries. Cut the canes of old plants down to the ground before new growth is well advanced.

■ **Plant perpetual strawberries** for fruit later this year. Remove the first flush of flower buds from summer-fruiting varieties planted in autumn and all buds from those put in now so plants build up strength.

■ **Divide alpine strawberries**, and sow new plants under glass. If conditions are warm, sow outdoors.

■ **Start early vines** under glass into growth.

■ **Cover strawberries** with cloches or polythene tunnels to advance their harvest by a few weeks.

■ **Prune trained fruit trees** such as apples, pears, plums, figs.

■ **Thin small fruits,** such as apricots and gooseberries, as well as wall-trained fruits.

■ **Uncover forced rhubarb** now that open-air supplies are plentiful; remove pots and boxes, and allow forced plants to recover without further picking.

■ **Tie in autumn-fruiting raspberry** canes as they develop. Thin them where necessary, keeping only the strongest spaced about 10cm (4in) apart along the wires.

■ **Keep gooseberries well watered** and mulched as a precaution against gooseberry mildew, which tends to be much worse in dry conditions.

■ **Net strawberries** to prevent birds from eating the ripening fruits.

■ **Pull out suckers** growing beside raspberries, gooseberries, apples and pears while they are small.

■ **Pollinate early blossom** on fruits grown in the greenhouse; use a soft paintbrush to transfer pollen by gently stroking the centre of each flower. Strawberries under glass may need the same assistance.

■ **Hand-pollinate outdoor** peaches, nectarines and apricots if the weather is too cold for bees and other pollinating insects.

Protecting blossom

Wall-trained fruits that flower early are more at risk from spring frosts than those in the open garden, because of the still conditions that prevail near boundaries and garden structures. Protect the blossom by draping plants with fleece or fine net curtains at night.

Strawberries need similar protection or covering with cloches. If the flowers do get frosted, it is possible to wash off the frost early, before the sunshine can damage the frozen blooms and turn the centres black.

■ **Fit a fine spray** attachment to a hosepipe or hand sprayer and mist the flowers until all signs of frost have gone.

Pruning

The purpose of pruning now is to improve the health of the fruit plants and ensure maximum cropping later on.

Bush and cane fruits Most new cane and bush fruits need formative pruning so that they grow into the desired shape. You can do this straight after planting, or wait until early in their first spring.

■ **Cut the canes** of raspberries, blackberries and hybrid berries to a bud 15–23cm (6–9in) above ground.

■ **Cut all stems** of blackcurrants to about 5cm (2in) high. Select the best four or five shoots that appear later and retain these; if these are less than 45–60cm (18–24in) long at the end of the season, cut growth back again next spring.

■ **Cut back all shoots** on gooseberries, red currants and white currants by half to an upward-pointing bud. Prune cordons and other trained forms by cutting back main branches by half, and all sideshoots to 2–3cm (1in). Remove all growth on the lower 10–15cm (4–6in) of the main stem to establish a clear 'leg'.

Apples and pears Remove any surplus new shoots from apple and pear trees trained as espaliers, cordons or fans.

■ **Cut back the ends** of branches on well-established trained trees and main stems to limit their extent.

■ **Pinch out flower** or fruit clusters on trees under two years old, to direct energy into new growth rather than the production of fruit.

Figs Hard-prune young trees to encourage branching; tie in new shoots as they develop.

■ **Remove any dead** or weak shoots on older trees, and cut

The blossom of peach trees trained against a wall is particularly vulnerable to damage by late frosts and may need protection with a covering of horticultural fleece.

Thin out any fruiting spurs on apple or pear trees that have become crowded or cross each other.

off the tips of main branches to stimulate fruiting sideshoots.

■ **Cut back a few of the old branches** to one or two buds, to encourage the formation of some young replacement stems.

Plums, peaches and cherries Prune stone fruits in growth because wounds heal faster than when dormant in winter; this reduces the risk of infection by silver-leaf disease.

■ **Cut out all dead,** diseased, injured and crossing or overcrowded branches.

■ **Remove any unwanted** new growth on espalier and fan-trained trees, particularly shoots growing towards the back or front of the tree.

Grapes Cut off the tip from each flowering shoot, two leaves beyond the first bunch of flowers.

■ **Pinch out the tip** of any sideshoots that are produced after one leaf.

■ **Tie in the flowering** shoots to training wires.

Silver-leaf is a fungus that affects plums and cherries; leaves turn silver, then brown, and infected branches die back.

Tying in berries

In mild gardens, the new stems of blackberries and hybrid berries are usually trained in autumn, after the old fruited canes are removed. However, in gardens where conditions are colder the young canes are loosely bundled along a wire for added protection. These can be untied in spring and the canes fanned out evenly on the wires; secure them with string or plastic twists. Very long canes can be cut off at the top wire. Alternatively, you can tie them along the wire or arch them above the supports, tying the tips to the top wire so that the stems form gentle loops.

Thinning gooseberries

1 Thin out the newly formed gooseberries when they are roughly the size of grapes.

2 Leave the fruits, or clusters of fruit, 5–8cm (2–3in) apart. You can use the thinnings for jam.

Thinning small fruits

Certain trees and bushes set excessively heavy crops of fruit, which are unlikely to reach good size and quality unless some are removed early.

■ **Thin trained peaches,** nectarines and apricots, especially those grown under glass, when the fruitlets are the size of hazelnuts. Reduce each cluster to a single fruit, and thin out the rest so that the fruitlets are spaced about 8–10cm (3–4in) apart along the branches.

■ **Thin gooseberries once** they are roughly the size of grapes so that single berries, or clusters of two or three, are spaced evenly along the stem (see below).

■ **Trained apples and pears** benefit from similar treatment towards the end of May.

Feeding and mulching

Once fruit has started growing, usually in April, use a general-purpose or high-potash feed in powdered or granular form.

■ **Sprinkle it over** a slightly larger area of soil than is shaded by stems or branches; lightly rake in.

■ **Water it in during periods** of dry weather. After two weeks, mulch with a 5–8cm (2–3in) layer of garden compost or well-rotted manure.

■ **For bush or cane fruit,** apply the powdered or granular feed at a rate of 70g (2oz) per plant.

■ **For trained fruit trees,** apply at a rate of 100g per m^2 (3oz per sq yd).

Plants growing in fruit cages

For an early crop of strawberries outdoors, cover plants with cloches in cold weather. On warm days ventilate freely, by removing some or all of the cloches. Water regularly and feed plants when they start flowering.

■ **Spread straw or lay mats** around strawberries to keep the fruits clean and dry. Wait to do this until the fruit-bearing stems begin to arch over, as it could prevent the soil from warming up and so delay ripening.

To ensure bunches of good-sized grapes form on your greenhouse or conservatory vines, you will need to thin out the developing fruits once they are about the size of a pea. Do this in April if your greenhouse is heated but postpone until summer in a cool greenhouse.

Mulch raspberries, using the first few cuts of lawn mowings (provided they haven't been treated with weed or moss killer).

■ **Spread a layer** of clippings 5–8cm (2–3in) thick on both sides of the rows; alternatively, use garden compost or leaf-mould.

Check blackcurrants for any overlooked big buds, conspicuous now as they remain lifeless or produce distorted flowers and leaves. Treat for big bud mite.

Bees and pollinating insects can fly through the holes in netting cages to pollinate your fruit, so there is no need to open cages specially for this.

Fruit under glass

Apricots, peaches and vines will be coming into flower in the greenhouse, while forced rhubarb and strawberries should be ready for picking. Discard rhubarb crowns after forcing, but plant strawberries in the garden after hardening off; they may crop again in late summer. Alpine strawberries make attractive plants, and sowing seeds under glass now is a good way to build up stocks of unusual varieties.

Pollinating Apricots, peaches and strawberries grown in the greenhouse often flower before many pollinating insects are about, especially if the weather is cold.

■ **Open wide the ventilators** and doors on warm days to allow early insects to fly in.

■ **If this is not possible,** you will need to take a soft paintbrush and stroke the centre of each bloom lightly to transfer the pollen from one flower to another, just as a bee would do. Do this around midday if possible.

■ **Early outdoor apricots** and peaches on warm walls may flower too early for insects and will benefit from hand pollination too.

Thinning In a mild season, early varieties can set a heavy crop of fruitlets by late March, and these should be thinned as soon as possible to ensure good-sized fruits.

- **Reduce clusters** to leave one or, at the most, two fruitlets in each.
- **Thin crowded** stems to leave a fruitlet every 5–8cm (2–3in). If all these develop, you should thin them further in late spring.

Greenhouse grapes

In unheated greenhouses, grape vines will be coming into leaf and flower, especially if the stems are sprayed every day or two with warm water to stimulate the buds to open. If you lowered the main stems in winter to encourage the buds to break evenly, you can retie them on their wires when the majority of buds show early leaf. In heated greenhouses and conservatories, the vines will be flowering now, so tap the stems every day with a cane to fertilise the flowers.

Thinning grapes

As trusses often set too many fruits, thin a heavy set when grapes are the size of small peas, to prevent the developing fruits from crowding each other. You may need to do this in April in a warm greenhouse, but wait until early summer in an unheated one.

- **Using a pair of pointed**, long-bladed scissors, remove most of the grapes in the centre of the bunch, and the smallest grapes around the point of the bunch, but leave plenty in the widest part or 'shoulders'; aim to leave at least a pencil thickness between the grapes.
- **Pinch out the shoots** at the second leaf beyond a truss of setting fruit.

Alpine strawberries

Using a soil-based compost, sow the seeds of alpine strawberries sparingly in trays or pots. Cover them thinly with more compost and keep them in a propagator or greenhouse at about 18°C (64°F) until seedlings appear. Prick these out individually into small pots when they have two true leaves, and plant out in May or June.

Many alpine strawberries do not make runners in the same way as large-fruited kinds, but instead grow into large clumps like a border perennial. Although these will fruit if left alone, yield and quality are greatly improved if you split large clumps into smaller segments every few years.

Scale insects

These minute sap-feeding insects can attack fruit trees and vines, especially those growing under glass. They shelter under waxy oval scales on shoots and branches where they lay their eggs safe from most insecticides, so you will have to remove them by hand (see below). Spraying with insecticide is effective only against the migrating juveniles, which usually emerge in early summer outdoors, but much earlier under heated glass.

- **Inspect stems closely** in warm spells during spring and summer and look for traces of the brownish oval scales that conceal the insects' eggs. Spray the minute crawling insects are seen.
- **Spray again a fortnight** later to catch survivors and late hatchings before they develop their protective scales.

Dealing with scale insects

1 Check plants in early spring for the brownish scales, particularly on the woody stems of vines, apricots and peaches.

2 Wipe them off using the end of a cotton bud or the tip of a folded soft cloth, dipped in alcohol.

Spring is a busy time in the kitchen garden and there are many varieties of vegetables, herbs and fruit that can be sown or planted out during this season. However there will also be some plants cropping now, such as overwintered vegetables or early salads.

Anise hyssop

Agastache foeniculum

The fresh aniseed-flavoured leaves of this short-lived perennial can be used to make teas and flavour cold drinks. Chop and add to savoury rice and meat dishes. Mauve summer flowers attract bees and butterflies. Pick the leaves and flowers for drying just as the buds open. Hardy.

Site Sun. Rich moist soil.

How to grow Sow seed indoors in spring. Replenish stock by taking soft or semi-ripe cuttings in August or divide in spring.

Asparagus

Asparagus officinalis

A perennial vegetable with succulent young shoots that grow from asparagus roots, or 'crowns'. Although expensive to buy, the plants will crop for many years. 'Fileas' is the earliest variety. Hardy.

Site Sun. Well-drained soil with plenty of well-rotted manure or compost added.

How to grow In mid-spring dig trenches with raised ridges at the bottom. Plant year-old crowns 30cm (12in) apart in the trench, spreading their roots on either side of the ridge. Space rows 45cm (18in) apart. Harvest when spears are 15cm (6in) high from mid-spring to early summer; it will be several years before the plants begin to crop well. Feed with a general fertiliser after harvesting is complete, and in autumn cut back top growth and top-dress with manure.

Broccoli, early sprouting

Brassica oleracea Italica Group

The immature flowering shoots of white or purple sprouting broccoli, available from January to the end of spring, are eaten lightly cooked. For continuity grow both early and late varieties or sow a prepared mixture. Hardy.

Site Sun, warm sheltered. Well-drained, non-acid soil.

How to grow Sow in April, thinly in rows in a nursery bed. Thin seedlings to 8cm (3in) apart, and in midsummer transplant 60cm (2ft) apart. Water well in dry weather. Cut

shoots when 8–10cm (3–4in) long with sprigs of young foliage. Harvest frequently to encourage new shoots.

Broccoli, late purple-sprouting

Brassica oleracea Italica Group

Grown for its leafy flowerheads, late purple-sprouting broccoli is a useful vegetable that follows on from the earlier cropping varieties. Hardy.

Site Sun. Fertile, moist and slightly acid soil.

How to grow Sow thinly into a seedbed in mid to late spring. Transplant in early summer to midsummer, allowing 45cm (18in) between each plant and row, and keep well watered until established. Protect from cabbage root fly by fitting 'collars' around the base of individual plants. Harvest from mid to late spring when the flowerheads are well formed but before the flowers begin to open. Pick off flowerheads regularly as production will cease if the flowers are left to develop.

Cabbage, spring

Brassica oleracea Capitata Group

Varieties such as 'Pixie' and 'Duncan' make small juicy cabbages, while 'Vanguard' and 'Wintergreen' are leafy non-hearting 'greens'. To maximise yields, harvest alternate plants while small, leaving others to grow and heart up. Hardy.

Site Sun, sheltered. Rich firm soil, with added lime if acid.

How to grow Sow two to three batches from early July to early August, thinly in rows in a nursery bed. Thin to 8cm (3in) apart, and transplant when seedlings are six weeks old, spacing hearted kinds 30cm (12in) apart each way, greens 25cm (10in) apart. Water well in dry weather and net against birds. In late winter feed with high-nitrogen fertiliser. Harvest as soon as large enough, leaving 5cm (2in) stumps to resprout.

Carrot, early

Daucus carota

Carrots can be sown under protection during late winter to provide an early crop in spring. Suitable varieties for an early crop include 'Minicor' (syn. 'Amsterdam Forcing', 'Baby Nantes'), 'Early Nantes' and 'Paris Market'. Hardy.

Site Sun. Well-drained and stone-free soil that has been manured but not during the past year.

How to grow Sow seed thinly under cloches or in frames, in rows 15cm (6in) apart. If necessary, thin seedlings to 5cm (2in) apart. Round-rooted varieties can be sown in a greenhouse, in modular trays with four seeds per cell, and planted out later. Plant out cell-grown clumps 15cm (6in) apart.

Keep well watered during dry spells. In spring when the cloche or frame is removed, cover with fleece to protect from carrot root fly. Harvest from late spring onwards.

Cauliflower, winter

Brassica oleracea Botrytis Group

Winter cauliflowers such as 'Armado April', 'Markanta' and richly coloured 'Purple Cape' are hardy varieties for mild areas.

Site Sun and sheltered. Firm, neutral to alkaline soil.

How to grow Sow in May, in rows in a nursery bed, and thin to 8cm (3in) apart. Transplant when seedlings have four to six true leaves, 75cm (2ft 6in) apart each way. Water in well and keep moist in dry weather. Protect forming heads by breaking some of the outer leaves to lie across the curds. Start cutting heads while still small, as whole batches tend to mature together.

Chinese basil (japanese shiso, perilla)

Perilla frutescens

The ruffled purple-red or green leaves of this annual herb have a warm curry-like flavour. It is an essential ingredient of sushi, but young leaves and flower stalks can also be used raw in salads or cooked in soups and pickles. Tender.

Site Sun or light shade. Well-drained soil.

How to grow Sow under glass in spring, and plant out 30cm (12in) apart after the last frosts. Pick growing tips regularly to encourage bushy growth.

Chives

Allium schoenoprasum

A clump-forming perennial herb with slender, grass-like green leaves that have a mild onion flavour. Spherical bright purple flowers are borne throughout summer. Chinese or Garlic chives (*A. tuberosum*) has broader, garlic-flavoured leaves and white flowers. Snipped chives are a useful garnish for salads, soups and sandwiches. Can also

be used as a border edging, container plant and for underplanting roses. Hardy.

Site Sun, partial shade. Fertile and moist but well-drained soil.

How to grow Sow seed outdoors in spring. Divide plants every 3–4 years in autumn. Ensure plants do not dry out, particularly when grown in containers.

Corn salad (lamb's lettuce)

Valerianella locusta

This mild salad annual has refreshing, slightly bitter leaves. It can be sown in spring for summer use, but is most valuable in the kitchen garden as a winter and early spring leaf crop. Hardy.

Site Sun or light shade. Most soils.

How to grow Sow outdoors in July and August, thinly in broad rows 15cm (6in)

wide. Thin seedlings to 10cm (4in) apart, transplanting some thinnings to a coldframe or greenhouse; select only the strongest seedlings. Keep moist at all times. Gather leaves or whole plants as required, first blanching plants under pots for one to two weeks if you find the flavour of the leaves is too bitter. Sowings may be left unthinned for harvesting as cut-and-come-again crops – snip strips to 2–3cm (1in) high.

Endive

Cichorium endivia

This annual or biennial crop is similar in appearance to a loose-leaved lettuce, but it has a sharper flavour. However, this is less pronounced if the plants are blanched. Curly-leaved varieties of endive are sown in spring for summer use, but hardy varieties, such as 'Golda', can be harvested in winter and early spring, especially if protected to maintain quality.

Site Sun, warm sheltered. Well-drained soil.
How to grow Sow in August and September, outdoors in a nursery bed or in modules under glass. Thin or transplant to 30cm (12in) apart each way. Water in dry weather. In exposed gardens and particularly cold conditions cloche crops or transplant seedlings to a coldframe. To blanch an endive and reduce the slight bitterness of the flavour, cover the plant with an upturned flowerpot or large plate around 10–14 days before you want to cut it.

Fennel

Foeniculum vulgare

A tall-growing perennial, fennel has soft green feathery foliage. In summer it bears flat heads of small yellow flowers, attracting hoverflies that eat aphids. Bronze fennel (*F. vulgare* 'Purpureum') is even more handsome. Fennel leaves are used to season meat and the seeds to flavour sauces and fish dishes. Hardy.
Site Sun. Well-drained, fertile soil.
How to grow Sow seed outdoors in spring. Divide in spring. Fennel self-seeds freely so harvest the seeds before they have a chance to scatter, or remove the flowers if seeds are not required.

Good King Henry (poor man's asparagus)

Chenopodium bonus-henricus

The early shoots of this undemanding perennial are blanched for cutting in early spring; later the green arrow-shaped leaves can be picked and used like spinach. Self-seeds freely, so deadhead to keep under control. Hardy.
Site Sun or light shade, sheltered spot. Well-drained soil.

How to grow Sow in spring in a nursery bed, thin to 10cm (4in) apart, then transplant in autumn to 45cm (18in) apart in each direction. Heap soil 15cm (6in) high over mature plants in autumn and cut shoots in spring as they emerge. Stop cutting and remove the soil mound in June, then mulch with compost. Divide plants every three to four years.

Leaf beet

Beta vulgaris Cicla Group

There are two main kinds of leaf beet: chard or seakale beet has thick stems and sculpted leaves, while perpetual spinach or spinach beet has large plain leaves that make a long-lasting weather-proof substitute for ordinary spinach, especially on drier soils. Hardy.
Site Sun or light shade. Fertile and well-drained soil.
How to grow Sow *in situ* in March or April, two to three seeds per sowing, 30cm (12in) apart each way. Sow again in August for transplanting to a coldframe for winter use. Water in dry weather and mulch well. Pick leaves as required or cut whole plants down to 2–3cm (1in). Water and feed with general fertiliser after a heavy picking.

Lemon balm, variegated

Melissa officinalis 'Aurea'

Grown for its wrinkled green leaves, which give off a lemon scent if crushed, lemon balm looks most attractive in spring when it forms low clumps of neat foliage. This variegated form is one of the most decorative, with green-and-gold leaves. Stems of pale yellow to white flowers, which are attractive to bees, are borne in summer. The leaves are used to make tea. Hardy.
Site Sun. Fertile and moist soil.
How to grow Sow seed indoors in spring. Grow on in pots and harden off before planting out. Can be invasive. In cold areas plants benefit from winter protection with fleece or straw.

Lettuce, overwintered

Lactuca sativa

Autumn-sown lettuce can be grown under the protection of cloches or frames or in an unheated greenhouse over winter to give a good spring crop. Select a hardy variety that is suitable for winter cultivation.

Site Sun. Fertile and well-drained soil.
How to grow Sow thinly under glass in rows 23cm (9in) apart from very late summer to mid autumn. Thin seedlings to 15–23cm (6–9in) apart. Ventilate when weather permits to avoid disease.

Mint (spearmint)

Mentha spicata

This is the most popular of the large and varied mint family. The long, toothed green leaves are borne along upright stems and clusters of mauve flowers appear in summer. Mint is a very invasive perennial, spreading by means of underground runners, so grow it in a large bottomless container sunk in the ground. The leaves are commonly used in mint sauce and drinks. Hardy.

Site Sun, partial shade. Any soil, except dry.

How to grow Sow seed outdoors or take root cuttings in spring. Divide at any time. Trim clumps regularly to limit spread.

Mustard and cress

Sinapsis alba and *Lepidium sativum*

These cut-and-come-again crops can be sown outdoors as an edging to a salad bed or as a catch crop between other vegetables. There are various kinds of cress, including Greek and finely cut leaved varieties. All cress seeds are sown two to three days before the mustard to ensure seedlings are ready together. Hardy.

Site Light shade. Moist soils.

How to grow Sow *in situ* every two to three weeks between March and October (November in a greenhouse border). Broadcast the cress seeds in drills 15–30cm (6–12in) wide or in patches and lightly rake in; oversow with mustard seeds two to three days later. Keep moist at all times. Cut with scissors when 5cm (2in) high, leaving short stumps to resprout.

Radish

Raphanus sativus

A quick-growing salad vegetable that can be grown as a late spring crop by sowing in winter under protection. The crisp peppery roots can be sliced into salads. Hardy.

Site Sun. Humus-rich and well-drained soil, not freshly manured.

How to grow Sow seed in mid to late winter under cloches or frames in rows 15cm (6in) apart, then thin seedlings to 2–3cm (1in) apart. Or, sow broadcast in a drill 10cm (4in) wide. For the best flavour, pull the radishes when the roots are no larger than 2–3cm (1in) in diameter.

Rhubarb

Rheum x *hybridum*

Rhubarb is classified as a vegetable but its stalks are eaten as a fruit. Its large green leaves are never eaten as they are highly poisonous. Rhubarb crops naturally during spring and early summer, but can be forced for a late winter crop. The variety 'Timperley Early' produces the earliest crops outdoors without being forced. Hardy.

Site Sun. Any soil, but preferably heavy and acid.

How to grow Plant new crowns in autumn or spring. Leave untouched for the first year and harvest only a little in the second. From then on, always leave three to four stems on the plant to avoid weakening it. Mulch with well-rotted compost or manure in winter.

Rosemary

Rosmarinus officinalis

An aromatic evergreen shrub with deep green, needle-like leathery leaves used for flavouring bread, meat, rice and egg dishes. The soft blue flowers are attractive to bees from mid-spring to early summer. There are many forms, including prostrate and variegated kinds. Leaves may be scorched after a cold winter. Plants usually recover if pruned back to healthy wood. Hardy.

Site Sun, sheltered. Well-drained soil.

How to grow Sow seed under glass in spring or take semi-ripe cuttings in mid to late summer. Trim after flowering and in early spring.

Salad rocket

Eruca vesicaria

An easy and useful leaf vegetable for salads, rocket has a delicious hot peppery flavour. It can be sown from late winter right through to autumn for harvesting almost all the year round. Hardy.

Site Sun. Fertile, moist but well-drained soil.

How to grow Sow in late summer for a very early crop the following spring. Allow 30cm (12in) between rows, and thin seedlings to 10cm (4in) apart. Keep plants well watered to avoid them running to seed early. In cold areas, protect plants over winter with cloches. Harvest frequently.

Seakale

Crambe maritima

This perennial, which grows wild by the sea, is blanched under pots for cutting in

early spring. It may be grown from seed or from root cuttings known as 'thongs'. Produces handsome flower and seed heads up to 60cm (2ft) across, which are popular with flower arrangers. Hardy.

Site Sun or light shade, sheltered. Light well-drained soil.

How to grow Sow in a nursery bed in spring, and thin seedlings to 15cm (6in) apart. Transplant seedlings or plant thongs 45cm (18in) apart the following spring. Water in dry weather and mulch. Force two-year-old plants in January, covering them with an upturned bucket or forcing pot – the tender, white 15–20cm (6–8in) shoots will be ready two months later. Feed with general fertiliser after forcing, and replace after five to six years with root cuttings.

Shallot

Allium cepa Aggregatum Group

These multiplier onions – each bulb splits to produce a cluster of four to ten new ones – have a distinctive, almost perfumed flavour. Traditional varieties were planted in autumn, but modern kinds bolt if started too early. Not fully hardy.

Site Sun. Rich, well-drained soil.

How to grow Plant virus-free bulbs 20cm (8in) apart in each direction in February or March, with their tips just showing. Water in dry weather and keep free of weeds. Gently lift clumps with a fork when leaves die down in midsummer, and leave to dry on the soil's surface. When the skins are papery and dry, separate bulbs and store them in nets or boxes in a cool, airy place for winter and spring use. Save smaller healthy bulbs to replant next year.

Sorrel

Rumex acetosa

A tall-growing plant, sorrel produces stems clothed with large, lance-shaped, mid-green leaves. In early to midsummer these are topped with inconspicuous greenish flowers that age to reddish brown. The plant has little decorative value, but the strongly flavoured leaves can be used sparingly in soups and omelettes and with meat; the young, more mildly flavoured foliage can be mixed into salads. Hardy.

Site Sun, partial shade. Acid, humus-rich and moist soil.

How to grow Sow seed outdoors in spring or divide plants in spring or early autumn. Remove flowerheads when they appear, as sorrel has a tendency to run to seed early. In warm areas grow in partial shade.

Spinach, summer

Spinacea oleracea

The flavour of well-grown spinach amply rewards the extra watering and mulching required. Start sowing this annual early in spring; on hot dry soils grow a bolt-resistant variety. Modern varieties crop all year with winter protection. Hardy.

Site Sun, but with light shade in midsummer. Mulch soil with plenty of added organic matter.

How to grow Sow *in situ* every four to five weeks from April to July, and thin seedlings to 15cm (6in) apart. Water regularly in dry weather and mulch with compost. Harvest when plants have five to six true leaves; cut whole plants to leave stumps for resprouting, or pick some larger leaves. Clear and freeze crops that start to bolt.

Spring onion (salad onion)

Allium cepa

These are young onion plants that are grown close together. If successive sowings are made, spring onions can be harvested over much of the year. Sow seed at fortnightly intervals from late winter to mid-summer. Hardy.

Site Sun. Well-drained and fertile soil, not freshly manured.

How to grow For a spring crop, sow thinly during midsummer, allowing 10cm (4in) between rows, or sow broadcast in a broad drill up to 10cm (4in) wide in a sheltered

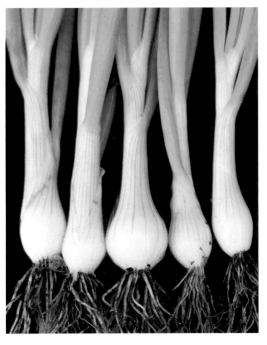

site. Water the drill before sowing in dry weather. Thin if necessary to 1–2cm (½–1in) apart. For the best flavour, pull onions before their bases swell.

Sweet cicely

Myrrhis odorata

Sweet aniseed-flavoured perennial that makes a mound of delicate foliage. Leaves, roots and seeds are all useful for flavouring salads, dressings, ice cream and fruit. Gather seeds for drying in late summer; alternatively, cut down after flowering for more young foliage. Hardy.

Site Light shade. Rich, well-drained soil.

How to grow Sow seed outside in early to mid spring; alternatively, leave to self seed or divide in autumn.

Sweet woodruff

Galium odoratum

Attractive ground-covering perennial with the scent of new-mown hay, used for

flavouring cold drinks, tisanes and fruit cups. Harvest the foliage as it appears, and flowers and stalks in early summer; dry to heighten their flavour. Hardy.
Site Light or semi-shade. Rich soil.
How to grow Sow seed in early spring or divide established plants.

Thyme

Thymus species and cultivars

There are many upright or creeping evergreen thymes, some variegated, with pink, purple or white summer flowers. All are ornamental aromatic plants, but grey-green garden thyme (*T. vulgaris*) is the most useful for the kitchen. Use fresh at any time for stuffings and bouquet garni. For drying, gather just before flowering. Hardy.
Site Sun. Poor, well-drained soil.
How to grow Sow seed under glass in early or mid spring or divide at this time. Layer in

summer or take semi-ripe cuttings in early summer. Trim after flowering. In very cold areas pot up and overwinter under cover.

Turnip

Brassica rapa

For summer use this mild crop is sown from spring onwards and harvested while the round or flat roots are still small and juicy. A winter-hardy variety, such as 'Manchester Market', can be sown late, and forced and blanched for an early spring crop of 'turnip tops'. Add lime to acid soil.
Site Sun, but with a little light shade in midsummer. Mulch soil with plenty of added organic matter.
How to grow Sow summer crops outdoors every three to four weeks from March to July, thinning seedlings to 10cm (4in) apart in rows 20cm (8in) apart. Water little and often, and mulch when plants are larger. Harvest roots when 5cm (2in) across. For 'tops', sow in September and leave unthinned; give a general feed in February and let tops grow in the open, or feed in them in January and cover with a ridge of soil 15cm (6in) high to force and blanch the young shoots.

Summer

The vegetable garden

Summer is a busy time in the garden but it's also very rewarding as many vegetables are ready to be picked. You'll need to plant later crops now and make sure you water well during fine, hot weather, if you want to enjoy a bumper harvest that extends throughout the year.

Summer is the time for the first beans to appear. Harvest the pods while still young to guarantee the best flavour.

Summer checklist

■ **Sow more seeds** for succession in drills (short single rows) or small blocks, to ensure a continuing supply of fresh vegetables later in the year.

■ **Thin seedlings in stages,** rather than all at once. If you have space, transplant a few strong thinnings elsewhere. Water the row after thinning to settle the soil so that the remaining plants grow rapidly.

■ **Watch for slugs and other pests** and diseases. Take action immediately.

■ **Sow beetroot, carrots,** courgettes, dwarf french beans, kohl rabi, lettuce, mangetout and peas, outdoor cucumbers, radish, runner beans, swedes and turnips if not already done.

■ **Transplant brussels sprouts** and winter cauliflowers if not already done.

■ **Harvest crops as they mature** and water as necessary.

■ **Hoe beds weekly** to kill weed seedlings as they emerge.

■ **Apply a mulch** of well-rotted compost or other organic matter around the base of plants that occupy the ground for several months, to control weeds and to help keep the soil moist. Leave space to hoe through the centre of each row.

■ **Control pests,** such as aphids and caterpillars, with sprays containing a non-persistent rapeseed oil at seven to ten day intervals, and cover plants with insect-proof mesh to deter root fly infestation.

■ **Pick off any discoloured leaves** and other plant parts showing early signs of disease.

■ **Cut down and burn** potato tops if leaves show brown markings, the signs of blight.

■ **Control caterpillars** by picking them off by hand or by spraying affected crops with the biological agent *Bacillus thuringiensis*, which can prove effective without the risk of leaving pesticide residues.

■ **Sow a green manure,** such as crimson clover, fenugreek or winter tares, after crops have been cleared; this helps improve soil texture and fertility. Alternatively, sow a follow-on crop of quick-maturing peas or french beans, both of which add nitrogen to the soil as well as providing an edible crop.

■ **Plant winter-cropping** cauliflower, cabbages and kale.

■ **Make successional sowings** of lettuce, spinach, spring onions and salad radishes.

Watering

Vegetables grow rapidly at this time of year, and plants require plenty of water to sustain them. Ideally, use a method to get water straight to the plant roots, rather than wastefully spraying it over the leaves. Use water efficiently, by applying generous amounts when the plants are going through the critical stages of development.

■ **Lay a seep hose** alongside plants, so water oozes onto the soil exactly where it is needed and loss due to evaporation is minimal. In this way, soil between the rows and pathways remains dry, and weed seeds are not encouraged to germinate.

■ **Seedlings and crops** recently transplanted or thinned need watering so that they do not dry out and their growth can continue unchecked, especially in dry weather. Do this daily for the first four to five days until they have stopped wilting, a sign that new roots have formed and become established.

■ **Leafy plants and crops** with soft, lush growth, such as celery, lettuce and spinach, as well as cabbages and cauliflowers, benefit from 4–5 litres per metre of row (1 gallon per yard) once a week.

■ **Plants with edible fruits,** such as courgettes, tomatoes, peas and beans, should not go short of water at flowering time and when the fruits or pods are starting to swell.

■ **Potatoes benefit** from a heavy soaking just as the tubers begin to form, which for

A Dutch hoe has a flat rectangular blade on a U-shaped mounting, attached to a long handle and set at a slight angle.

a number of cultivars coincides with the start of flowering. Watering at this stage increases the overall yield significantly.

■ **Water sweetcorn** when the silks (tassels) on the small cobs have just started to shrivel, and again about 10 days before the cobs are due to be picked.

■ **The very firm planting** of brussels sprouts, required to prevent them from falling over as they grow, means that they rarely need water unless the weather is extremely dry.

Controlling weeds

Hoeing the soil with a Dutch hoe is the most effective way to control weeds in the vegetable patch, but it must be done with care so as not to disturb your cropping plants and seedlings.

■ **Run the hoe blade** just below the surface, no deeper than 1cm (½in), and push and pull it to and fro. This severs seedling weeds from their roots and minimises moisture loss and soil disturbance, which in turn helps to prevent more weed seeds from germinating.

■ **Hoe on a hot,** sunny day, so that weeds quickly wilt and die.

■ **In wet conditions** rake off the weeds or they will reroot. Leafy annual weeds can be added to the compost heap.

Watering guide

To increase yields apply water generously when plants reach the following stages in development:

Crop	When to water
Peas and beans	At flowering and when the pods begin to swell
Onions	As the bulbs start to develop
Carrots, turnips and other roots	As they begin to swell
Potatoes	When the tubers begin to form
Courgettes, marrows and squashes	At flowering and when the fruits start to swell
Sweetcorn	As the silks start to shrivel and 10 days before due to pick

Crops in summer

Summer is the time when you can begin to enjoy the fruits of your labours, with many plants ready to harvest now. There are still varieties to be planted to ensure crops later in the year.

Peas and beans In early June plant out runner beans 15cm (6in) apart in rows 60cm (2ft) apart. Make further sowings of dwarf french beans at three-week intervals. Space seeds 15cm (6in) apart in rows 20cm (8in) apart, as well as using them to fill in the gaps of any plants that failed to grow.

■ **Harvest peas sown in spring** when the pods are well developed but before they become tightly packed with seeds.

■ **Sow early pea varieties** for harvesting in late summer and maincrop varieties for harvesting in autumn. Sow in a broad drill at three-week intervals. Space the seeds 3–5cm (1–2in) deep in two or three rows 8cm (3in) apart.

Harvesting now

Summer is a time of plenty and the following crops are ready for eating now:

■ Asparagus	■ Japanese onions
■ Asparagus peas	■ Kohl rabi
■ Aubergines	■ Lettuces
■ Baby sweetcorn	■ Salad leaves
■ Beetroot	■ Peas and mangetout
■ Broad beans	■ Radish
■ Broccoli	■ Shallots
■ Calabrese	■ Spinach
■ Chard	■ Spinach beet
■ Chillies	■ Spring onions
■ Courgettes	■ Summer cabbage
■ Early carrots	■ Summer cauliflower
■ Early potatoes	■ Summer squash
■ Florence fennel	■ Sweetcorn
■ French beans	■ Sweet peppers
■ Runner beans	■ Tomatoes
■ Globe artichokes	■ Turnips

■ **Harvest peas sown** in early summer regularly while the pods are young, bright green and juicy. This encourages further yields and ensures tender peas of good quality. Peas will stop flowering if the pods are left on the plant.

■ **Harvest french beans** and runner beans every two to three days, and before the seeds start to swell prominently and the pods become stringy and tough.

Cabbage family It is time to transplant some brassicas. Do this firmly to prevent them from drying out and to help their root systems establish.

■ **Transplant savoy and winter** cabbages to their growing positions at a minimum spacing of 30 x 30cm (12 x 12in), for harvesting from late autumn through to mid spring. Closer spacing will result in more but smaller heads.

■ **Harvest summer cabbages** when they have developed a good solid heart. Use a sharp knife to cut through the main stem just above the oldest leaves. Leave stalks in the soil and make two cross cuts at right angles; new leaves will sprout from this stump to produce a crop of greens later in the year.

■ **Summer cauliflowers** are ready to harvest once the heads have swollen and the outer protective leaves open to show the white curd inside. Cut the head first, then clear the remaining stem and outer leaves.

■ **Cut broccoli before the flowers** show. Remove the central head with about 15cm (6in) of stem. This encourages smaller sideshoots to develop for harvesting later.

■ **Finish planting winter** and spring cauliflowers in July and space them 75cm (2ft 6in) apart in rows 75cm (2ft 6in) apart to give them plenty of growing room.

■ **Transplant winter cabbage** early in the season at a spacing of 50cm (20in) in rows 50cm (20in) apart. Choose the hardier 'January King' types for colder or more exposed areas.

Summer cabbages are ready to harvest. If you cut the stem you leave behind (see left) you wil get a crop of greens later in the year.

■ **Transplant kale** into its cropping site in July, spacing plants 45cm (18in) apart in rows 60cm (2ft) apart. The purple forms of kale tend to be less hardy than the green leaf forms.

■ **Earth up the soil** around the base of sprouting broccoli plants to a depth of about 15cm (6in). This helps to prevent them from falling over during winter if they become at all top-heavy.

■ **Sow spring cabbages** in seedbeds outdoors, with a second sowing 10 days later. Grow them as 'hearted' cabbages or cut as spring greens. Transplant spring cabbages sown in early summer, spacing plants 30cm (12in) apart in rows 30cm (12in) apart.

■ **Sow chinese cabbage** in July or August. Transplant seedlings sown in modules at a spacing of 30cm (12in) in rows 45cm (18in) apart. When colder weather comes, be prepared to protect them from frost in all but the mildest areas.

■ **Be vigilant for caterpillars** and mealy cabbage aphids, which can be a problem at this time, especially on broccoli. Hand-pick caterpillars or control both pests with spray containing a non-persistent rapeseed oil at seven to ten day intervals.

Onion family By now the onion relatives, shallots, sun-ripened and firm, are ready to lift. Shallots planted in winter are ready for harvesting as early as late June if the weather has been warm, dry and sunny. Summer sunshine ripens the bulbs as well as extending their storage life.

■ **Lift clumps of shallots** with a border fork as the leaves die down. Allow the bulbs to dry in the sun.

■ **Store shallot bulbs** once the skins are thoroughly dry and the remains of the tops pull off easily. Lay the bulbs in wooden or cardboard trays in a dry, cool, dark, frost-free place until required; shallots should keep for up to a year in the right conditions.

■ **Leeks sown in spring** are ready to transplant when they are about 20cm (8in) tall. Lightly trim off the tops of the leaves and the bottoms of the roots, and drop each young plant into a 15cm (6in) deep hole made with a dibber. Space holes 15cm (6in) apart. Water each plant. There is no need to firm as the soil soon collapses in around the roots, filling the hole.

You should be able to lift onions now; leave them on the soil to dry out but move indoors if rain threatens.

Earthing up potatoes

To earth up maincrop potatoes, rake the loose soil from the centre of each row around the potato plants, covering the bottom half of each stem. Make sure the soil is in close contact with each stem and the stems are emerging from the top of a ridge of soil. Firm the sides of the ridge with a spade blade and leave the top flat so that rain can soak down to the plant roots.

■ **Lift onions as soon as the tops** have died down. Ease them out of the ground gently, using a fork so as not to damage the roots, and leave them lying on the soil to dry out; they are ready to store when the skins turn papery. If the weather is wet, remove them to the greenhouse staging or take indoors until the weather improves.

■ **Continue to sow spring** onions at three-week intervals for successional crops.

■ **Sow next year's japanese** onions thinly in August or September about 1cm (½in) deep in rows 30cm (12in) apart. Sow them in the evening in a well-watered seedbed, as they germinate better in a cool soil.

■ **Lift japanese onions** which have been growing through the winter. Allow the tops to die back, and leave the bulbs in the ground so that the skins ripen before they are dug up.

Potatoes It is time to enjoy the first crop of new potatoes; the most reliable indication that early potatoes are ready for harvesting is when the flowers have opened.

■ **Lift early potatoes** with a border fork. Drive the fork under the ridge and gently shake the soil to expose the tubers. Harvest only what you need and use them as fresh as possible, leaving the rest of the crop growing until required.

■ **If potato blight** has been a problem in previous years, cut off and dispose of the leaves and stems, and harvest the entire crop early to prevent the disease re-establishing or spreading.

■ **In warm, humid conditions,** spray potatoes with a copper-based or other suitable fungicide. This may prevent potato blight becoming established. Completely coat both sides of the leaves for it to be effective.

■ **Meanwhile, earth up** maincrop potatoes when the plants are about 25cm (10in) high (see left), but first hoe between the rows to loosen the soil surface and remove any weeds. Earthing up keeps the young tubers moist and growing rapidly. More important, it prevents them from turning green and becoming poisonous.

■ **Water maincrop potatoes** thoroughly as the tubers are forming. The tubers of healthy plants can be harvested in autumn.

Kohl rabi is ready after about eight weeks; purple-skinned varieties take a little longer to mature than those with green skins.

Summer is the time when early potatoes are ready; ease a fork under the plants and agitate the soil until the potatoes are revealed.

Root crops There are types of root vegetable sown during summer. Make several small sowings every few weeks to spread harvesting over a long period. This method of successional sowing goes a long way towards avoiding the peaks and troughs in availability caused by changeable weather during the growing season. Another way to avoid gluts and gaps is to thin in stages, first harvesting baby vegetables to leave more growing space for later, larger roots.

■ **Sow kohl rabi** at three-week intervals throughout early summer. Sow seed 1cm (½in) deep and thin to a final spacing of 20cm (8in) apart in rows 30cm (12in) apart. Green-skinned types take seven to eight weeks from sowing to harvest, and mature faster than those with purple skins.

■ **Baby turnips** are ready to eat six weeks after sowing. Try out different cultivars by sowing a different one every three weeks throughout summer. Sow seed 2–3cm (1in) deep and thin to a final spacing of 15cm (6in) apart in rows 25cm (10in) apart.

■ **Sow round beetroot** at three-week intervals until mid July. Sow seed 2–3cm (1in) deep and thin to a final spacing of 5–8cm (2–3in) apart in rows 30cm (12in) apart; baby beets are ready to pull in eight to ten weeks.

■ **Carrots sown late** in June are less vulnerable to carrot fly than earlier sowings. Sow seed 1cm (½in) deep, and thin to 10cm (4in) apart in rows 15cm (6in) apart. Extend the harvest by sowing early varieties, ready in eight weeks, then maincrop varieties, which mature in 10–12 weeks.

■ **Harvest immature** turnips and carrots as baby vegetables, as they are required. You can combine this with thinning if you leave thinning until later than normal, so the roots have had a chance to develop. The remaining plants will then have space to develop full-size roots for later harvesting.

■ **Try not to disturb** carrots more than you need while thinning or harvesting as this releases a scent attractive to carrot root flies. To prevent flies from laying eggs, protect rows of young carrots with insect-proof netting tucked securely in the soil.

■ **Sow carrots** in July for a late crop of finger-sized roots.

■ **Sow turnips** during early August for winter use.

■ **Sow florence** fennel in July, 1cm (½in) deep, and thin seedlings in stages to 30cm (12in) apart in rows 40cm (16in) apart. You can also sow a little later, but these plants should be protected with cloches in September. Fennel sown at this time should produce good quality plants, but they rarely develop into large bulbs as autumn approaches and the days grow shorter.

■ **Sow hardy winter radishes** for harvesting over winter. Sow seeds thinly to give the seedlings plenty of room for the large roots to develop. Thin to a final spacing of 15–20cm (6–8in) in rows 25cm (10in) apart, depending on the variety of radish and size of roots required.

Perennial crops Pick globe artichokes from established plants when they are plump and just about to open. Cut them with about 15cm (6in) of stem, to encourage secondary, smaller heads to develop three to six weeks later.

■ **Feed globe artichoke** plants after harvesting the first crop. Apply a liquid fertiliser round the base of the plants and repeat two or three times at 10-day intervals; this will improve the size and quality of a second crop.

■ **Harvest late varieties** of rhubarb by cutting through the stalks at ground level.

Salad crops Keep up the supply of quick-maturing salad leaves by sowing in small batches at two to three-week intervals. Ensure that while one crop is ready for picking, others are at different stages of maturity. Sow seed 1cm (½in) deep.

■ **Thin lettuces** in stages to 25cm (10in) apart in rows 30cm (12in) apart. Do not transplant thinnings in hot, dry weather as they will run straight to seed.

■ **Harvest cut-and-come-again** crops like lettuces and spinach regularly or they may run to seed.

■ **Sow radishes** and spring onions in short rows, so as not to produce more than you need. Sow seed 1cm (½in) deep and very thinly indeed.

■ **Continue to water** at regular intervals if there is no rain, so that leafy salad crops like rocket do not run to seed.

■ **Continue to sow** spinach at two-week intervals. Choose rough-seeded cultivars at this time of year as they are hardier than those with smooth seeds.

■ **Sow chicory in beds** for transplanting later. Choose the sugar-loaf types as they can tolerate light frost. They will crop through winter if you protect plants with cloches or a straw mulch in severe weather.

■ **Sow spinach beet** for early spring harvest. Make two or three sowings at three-week intervals. Sow seed 2cm (¾in) deep and thin plants to 15cm (6in) apart in rows 30cm (12in) apart. Be prepared to protect the plants in winter if the site is cold and exposed.

■ **Water celery** during dry periods, giving at least 1 litre (2 pints) per plant per week. Keep the plants growing rapidly and the sticks soft and succulent by applying a liquid feed of organic nitrogen every two weeks when you water.

If you have a small garden you can still grow vegetables: a simple raised bed can produce a respectable crop of lettuce.

Planting sweetcorn

Plant sweetcorn seedlings in blocks, with each plant 35cm (14in) apart. When they grow, the wind will help pollination between the plants far more effectively than if they were set in rows.

Tender crops It is safe to plant tender crops in colder areas now that the danger of frost has passed. Do this early in June to provide them with as long a growing season as possible.

■ **Plant tomatoes and peppers** outside now into growing bags or fertile soil. Feed and water regularly.

■ **Support tall-growing** cordon tomatoes and peppers with a stout cane driven in close to each plant. Tie in the stems at intervals of 20–30cm (8–12in). Use raffia or soft string to avoid bruising the delicate stems and do not tie too tightly (especially near the base) as this could constrict the stem as it swells.

■ **Plant out sweetcorn** plants 35cm (14in) apart in blocks (not rows), to aid pollination by the wind (see left).

■ **Harvest immature** 'mini-corns' from sweetcorn sown under cloches in May or in pots indoors in April. Cut off these young, unpollinated cobs when they are about 10cm (4in) long; the plants are too soft for them to be pulled off like mature cobs.

■ **Cobs are mature** when the tassels on the ends have turned brown and the cobs are at an angle of 45 degrees to the plant's main stem. To be sure that sweetcorn is ready to harvest, press a thumbnail into a kernel – if the sap is creamy it is ready, if clear it is not.

■ **Sow courgettes,** marrows and ridge cucumbers in well-drained fertile soil. Dig holes 1.2m (4ft) apart, as deep and as wide as a spade blade. Half-fill with well-rotted organic matter and then top with soil to leave a slight mound. Sow three seeds onto the top of each mound; they should germinate in seven to ten days. Allow only

Holiday care for vegetables

Before you go on holiday, water all plants thoroughly and take the following precautions:

- Sink pipes or plant pots close to the base of larger plants, such as artichokes, to make watering easier and get the moisture down to the plant roots.
- Lay a seep hose along the rows or beds of vegetables and link it up to a timing device set to water plants automatically.
- Remove flowers from crops that may set seeds or develop fruits while you are absent. This is important if no one is harvesting your crops while you are away.

- Lay an organic mulch around wide-spaced plants, such as cabbages, to retain moisture and suppress weeds.
- Arrange for a friend or neighbour to visit your garden and harvest the vegetables as they mature, particularly the peas, beans, peppers and tomatoes.
- Arrange for them to water plants, particularly root crops. Carrots often split when subjected to irregular watering, and potatoes will stop swelling if the soil becomes too dry.

the strongest seedling to grow to maturity and remove the other two.

■ **Plant squashes and pumpkins** in well-drained fertile soil, prepared as described for courgettes and marrows.

■ **Train squashes** to prevent their vigorous stems becoming a tangled mass. Remove the tip of the main stem once five leaves have developed. This will encourage four or five sideshoots to sprout; as they grow spread them out like the spokes of a wheel.

■ **Hand-pollinate** squash and pumpkin flowers to ensure good cropping, especially in cool summers. The plants have separate male and female flowers and will produce fruits only if they are cross-pollinated. You can recognise the female by the tiny fruit behind the flower; male flowers have only a thin stalk. Remove one male flower and gently pull off the petals. Push the remaining flower part into the centre of a female flower to transfer the pollen; one male flower can pollinate up to four females.

■ **For large squash or pumpkins,** allow only one flower to develop on each stem, and remove all flowers once the required number of fruits start to form.

■ **Pick tomatoes** as they ripen. If the weather is wet, pick the fruits just before they are ripe rather than leave them on the plant for too long, as they may split.

■ **Harvest peppers** and chillies when the fruits are swollen and the skin smooth. Cut them from the plant with a small stalk attached when green, or leave them until fully ripe and coloured.

■ **Harvest aubergines** when the fruits are swollen and the skin is clear and glossy, but before the flesh inside becomes soft.

■ **Gather courgettes** as soon as they reach the required size. If they are left too long the plants will stop producing flowers and cropping will be interrupted.

■ **Continue to train** pumpkins and squashes by nipping out any new sideshoots. Pinch out the tips of existing sideshoots once a fruit has started to develop.

Storing vegetables

One of the main problems at this time of year is what to do with surplus produce. All too often, the sign of a successful season for a particular crop is over-production. Rather than trying to eat your way through everything, consider which crops can be

Potatoes can be stored in paper bags or hessian sacks; keep them in a cool dark cupboard or cellar. Make sure the environment is dry since damp conditions will cause your crop to rot.

stored. Those harvested young and succulent are ideal for freezing, and gluts of almost any vegetable can be turned into delicious chutneys and pickles. Then you have the double satisfaction of enjoying produce out of season and knowing that you grew and preserved it yourself. After harvesting, inspect your produce and freeze or store only that which is in perfect condition.

The best store is a cellar, basement, unheated room or shed where it is cool, dry and inaccessible to mice. It needs to be dark, airy and, ideally, fitted with slatted shelves to keep the produce off the floor. You need wooden boxes or cardboard boxes lined with newspaper for storing root vegetables, net

If you have a bountiful crop of beans you can store any that you don't eat immediately by freezing or drying.

Blanching involves immersing the prepared vegetables in boiling water for less than a minute, then plunging them into cold water and draining thoroughly. The best way to freeze is to spread the prepared vegetables in a single layer on a tray and open-freeze them, before putting them into plastic bags.

Peas and beans Freeze french and runner beans whole, after topping and tailing them, or sliced.

■ **Remove peas and broad beans** from their pods and freeze them as soon as possible after picking.

■ **For dried peas and beans,** lift whole plants laden with mature pods and hang them up to dry slowly in a cool, dry place, before removing the seeds from the pods. Store the dry seeds in sealed plastic containers or in coloured glass jars; keep them in a cool, dark room.

Cabbage family Freeze broccoli (calabrese) and sprouting broccoli as small florets or sideshoots.

bags for onions, marrows and pumpkins, and hessian or paper sacks for potatoes. Keep insulating materials such as straw, old blankets, rugs or newspapers handy in case temperatures fall. Check your stored produce every few weeks to see that there is no sign of decay.

A glut of vegetables can be easily turned into delicious preserves, be they pickles or chutneys; they make ideal gifts at Christmas.

■ **Slice or shred** cabbage and freeze; red cabbage also makes a tasty pickle.

■ **Winter cabbages** will keep well in the ground, or for two to three weeks after picking, suspended in a net in a cool, dry, dark place such as a shed.

■ **Although brussels sprouts** and kale can be frozen, there is little point as they are hardy plants and are better left in the ground for picking fresh, as required, from late summer through to winter.

Onion family Bulb onions, shallots and garlic are grown with storage in mind. After lifting, leave the crop to dry so that the sun cures the skins. This will seal in the nutrients and improve the storage qualities.

■ **Once dry, store the bulbs** in a dry, dark, cool but frost-free place such as a shed or garage. Leave them loose in a box or rack, hang in net bags, or tie into strings, with the tops tied or plaited together with string.

■ **Small onions** and shallots can be pickled.

Potatoes Maincrop potatoes keep quite well in the ground once they reach maturity. It is only as the weather gets colder and the soil becomes wetter that it is necessary to lift them. This may be well into autumn, unless the ground is required for other crops. But in a very wet September, or if blight has affected your potatoes, it is advisable to lift them early. After the skins have dried, store them in thick paper sacks to exclude light.

Root crops Many roots are safe left in the ground during a mild winter, especially if the soil is light and free-draining. It is a good idea to cover them with straw or bracken against the occasional hard frost. On heavy soils, and for easy access if the ground is frozen, many roots can be dug up and stored in a cool, frost-free place in paper or hessian sacks or cardboard boxes lined with newspaper. Do not wash before storing.

■ **Maincrop carrots** can be stored in boxes of damp sand. Early carrots will keep in a plastic bag in the fridge for two to three weeks, after cutting their tops off.

■ **Parsnips taste best** after frost has enhanced their aromatic sweetness, so leave in the soil until needed. Mark the end of the rows with a cane as all top growth disappears from sight.

■ **Turnips and swedes** are best left in the ground until needed.

■ **Beetroot** may be left in the ground for use as required or dug up in autumn and stored in damp sand, like carrots. Alternatively, it can be pickled in vinegar.

■ **Kohl rabi** will keep in the fridge for two to three weeks.

Salad and tender crops Many salad and fruiting crops can be frozen (see chart right), though some, like tomatoes and peppers, will only be suitable for cooking. Green tomatoes can be made into chutney.

■ **Store marrows** and pumpkins in a cool, dry, dark room once the skins have been allowed to 'ripen', or harden, in the sun.

■ **Lettuce and salad leaves** must be eaten fresh. Drench them in icy water and leave to drain, to preserve their freshness.

To freeze a glut of beans, blanch briefly and then allow to cool. Spread on a tray and freeze before transferring to freezer bags.

Preserving vegetables

Much of the wide array of vegetables that can be raised in the kitchen garden can be stored for later use, although different crops require different preserving methods.

Vegetable	Preserving method
Asparagus	Blanch and freeze spears
Aubergine	Slice or dice, blanch and freeze
Beetroot	Store dry; freeze baby beets whole
Broad beans	Pod beans, blanch and freeze; dry
Broccoli	Blanch and freeze florets
Cabbage	Slice or shred, blanch and freeze
Carrots	Slice or dice, blanch and freeze
Baby carrots	Whole; store in damp sand
Cauliflower	Blanch and freeze florets
Celery	Slice or dice, blanch and freeze
Chillies	Hang up to dry, threaded together
Courgettes	Slice or dice, blanch and freeze
French beans	Top and tail pods, blanch and freeze; dry
Garlic	Store dry
Kohl rabi	Slice or dice, blanch and freeze
Marrows	Store dry
Onions	Store dry
Parsnips	Leave in ground; slice, blanch and freeze
Peas	Pod, blanch and freeze; dry
Potatoes	Store dry in thick paper sacks
Pumpkin	Store dry
Runner beans	Slice, blanch and freeze; dry
Spinach	Blanch and freeze whole leaves
Sprouting broccoli	Blanch and freeze main shoots and sideshoots
Swede	Leave in ground; store dry
Sweetcorn	Strip off husks and silks; blanch and freeze whole cobs or kernels
Sweet peppers	De-seed, slice or chop and freeze
Tomatoes	Chop and freeze
Turnips	Leave in ground; store dry

Herbs are at their most flavoursome in summer so take advantage of this and use them fresh in your cooking. Watch out for vigorous herbs, like mint, and check their growth if they become invasive. As the season draws to a close, collect the seeds of herbs that have culinary uses and dry for winter use.

Summer checklist

■ **Nip out the growing tips** of bushy herbs, such as basil, savory and marjoram, to encourage plenty of new sideshoots.

■ **Thin or prick out** seedlings sown in late spring before they are too large, and pot up a few for the kitchen windowsill.

■ **Plant out tender herbs,** such as basil and lemon verbena, into permanent positions as soon as late frosts are over and young plants are acclimatised to outdoor conditions.

■ **Water recently planted herbs** in dry weather, and check those in containers regularly. Chervil, parsley, coriander and sorrel need regular watering, but avoid over-watering basil.

■ **Keep on top of weeds,** especially in new herb beds and borders.

■ **Pinch out parsley flowers** forming now on older plants to encourage more leaves, but allow one or two to flower and self-sow to provide seedlings that you can transplant in autumn.

■ **Shear off the flowerheads** of marjoram and other bushy herbs to encourage new leafy growth and to prevent seeds setting.

■ **Gather and dry flowerheads** of chamomile, hyssop and sweet woodruff, as well as lavender and pot marigolds (*Calendula*), to add colour to potpourri.

■ **Feed herbs** in containers and perennial herbs planted outside this year, using a high-potash fertiliser.

■ **Harvest herbs** while at their best. Pick small sprigs regularly for immediate use, larger quantities for preserving.

■ **Gather herbs** for preserving on a dry morning, ideally when it is slightly cloudy or before the sun reaches the plants. Harvest only as much as you can deal with

Many herbs, such as sage and thyme, can be grown in pots and make a valuable addition to patios and decking during summer.

Dry the flowers of pot marigolds and add to potpourri for a splash of bright colour and a distinctive scent.

straightaway and select only clean, healthy growth. Keep different herbs separate at all times to avoid cross-flavouring.

■ **Water and feed herbs** after each mass harvest. Annuals should regrow to supply a second harvest later in the summer and perennials will give another cut or two.

■ **Take soft cuttings** of marjoram, mint, rosemary, sage, thyme and tarragon, and leave to root in a propagator or in a pot on a warm windowsill.

■ **Layer low branches** of thyme and rosemary by pinning them down in the soil, but keeping the tips above ground. They should have rooted by winter.

■ **Pot on rooted cuttings** taken earlier in the summer.

■ **Prick out seedlings** from sowings made earlier in summer, and pot up any needed for indoor use over winter.

■ **Continue sowing parsley,** chervil and winter purslane for winter harvesting, indoors or in a coldframe.

■ **Gather seed heads** as they near maturity and dry the seeds for storing or sowing.

■ **Clear leaves and old foliage** from around plants that are being left to self-sow, and lightly loosen the soil as a seedbed.

■ **Begin tidying** the herb garden in September, deadheading or trimming tall plants and clearing exhausted annual herbs.

■ **Prepare the ground** for new herb beds and borders early in September, ready for planting in early autumn.

■ **Cut back tarragon** by half to stimulate young growth for late harvest or cuttings.

■ **Select strong** or bushy plants of chives, parsley and marjoram to pot up later for winter use. Feed them now with a high-potash fertiliser and water in dry weather to maintain quality. You can also lift a few parsley and basil plants and replant in a coldframe or greenhouse border to re-establish before autumn.

■ **Take semi-ripe** cuttings of non-flowering shoots of shrubby herbs such as cotton lavender, hyssop, lavender, rosemary, sage, thyme and winter savory.

Flowers and seeds

When herbs start to produce flowers you will need to decide whether to leave or remove them. Leave the flowers on those herbs grown for their culinary seeds, such as coriander or fennel, or on any where you wish to gather seed for sowing. Remove the flowers of any herbs that set seed freely and which can be invasive. Cutting off flowers can also promote bushy growth.

Mint planted in a vegetable plot or flower bed can become invasive. Growing it in a pot will confine its spread.

Mint

Most mints are vigorous and spreading. To prevent their running roots from invading neighbouring plants, plant them in an old bucket or plastic bag, or grow in a pot; make sure the container has plenty of drainage holes in the bottom and plunge it in the border soil.

■ **Trim back** any wandering roots once or twice during summer.

■ **As mint starts** to flower in July, the quality of the foliage deteriorates. So cut down a proportion of the tall stems to just above soil level, water well and feed with a high-nitrogen fertiliser to stimulate a second crop of young, full-flavoured leaves.

■ **Watch for mint rust**, distinguished by pale, swollen or distorted stems that later develop dirty orange spots on the leaves. Cut off all affected growth to ground level and burn or dispose of it promptly.

Basil

To grow well basil needs warmth and shelter, a free-draining rich soil and regular feeding. For these reasons do not plant or sow outdoors until after the last frosts. For a longer cropping period grow basil in a fertile greenhouse border or in 15–20cm (6–8in) pots of soil-based compost with a layer of coarse grit in the bottom for better drainage.

■ **Stand the pots** in a warm, sunny corner, protected from the wind.

■ **Water before midday** whenever the compost is dry, but avoid overwatering.

■ **Feed every** 10–14 days with high-nitrogen liquid fertiliser.

■ **Pinch out** the growing tips regularly, starting while the plants are still small, to encourage bushy growth and prolong the life of the plants by suppressing flowering.

Propagation

A variety of herbs are sown at this time, including a final and generous sowing of parsley for use in autumn from the open garden. With care this sowing should also see you through the winter – some plants can be potted up in September and grown under cover or indoors.

Semi-ripe cuttings

Propagate lavender and other woody herbs by taking semi-ripe cuttings. Pull off a 10cm (4in) long sideshoot with a 'heel' of tissue at the base. Remove all except the top five to ten leaves and dip the bases of the cuttings in hormone powder; shake off any excess. Make holes in a pot of soil or cuttings compost using a dibber. Insert the cuttings, 5cm (2in) deep, and water in well. Cover with a cloche or place in a propagator until rooted.

■ **Sow parsley** seeds sparingly in rows in a warm, sheltered part of the garden in mid July. When the seedlings are large enough to handle, water well and thin out to leave plants 8cm (3in) apart. Water again to firm.

■ **Sow basil** outside once the danger of frost has passed.

■ **Continue to sow** annual herbs, such as chervil, dill and coriander, outdoors, to ensure a continuous harvest all season.

■ **Sow chives,** fennel, winter savory and other biennials and perennials under glass or in a seedbed outdoors.

■ **Lift mature clumps** of mint after flowering and chop them into pieces with a spade. Transplant the younger, outer pieces into a fresh site, where they will grow more vigorously. Discard the exhausted central portion.

■ **Take semi-ripe** cuttings of shrubby herbs during July. Choose healthy, non-flowering shoots that are starting to turn woody. Cut a shoot just above a leaf joint. The sideshoots of lavender, hyssop and rosemary will provide suitable material.

Finely chop herbs like parsley and mint (left) and place in ice-cube trays. Top up with water and pop in the freezer.
Place the flowers of herbs like borage (right) in ice-cube trays and fill with water; freeze. Use the frozen flowers in summer drinks.

Harvesting herbs

Many herbs reach perfection around midsummer, when their foliage is still fresh and unblemished, and their flavour peaks just before flowering. This is the time to harvest large quantities to preserve for winter use.

Freezing This is the best way to preserve the full flavour and colour of most leafy culinary herbs. Freeze singly or in mixtures for convenience.

■ **Pick small sprigs** of foliage, wash in cold water and shake well. Do not pat them dry, as this can bruise the leaves. Place small bunches loosely in plastic bags and freeze. When fully frozen crush the leaves in their bags, working quickly

It's easy to oven-dry herbs such as rosemary and thyme. Try using the same method (see page 56) for sage and mint.

before they thaw, and pack the bags in a labelled container to save space.

■ **Chop leaves** finely after washing and pack them into the sections of ice-cube trays. Top up with water and freeze. Store the cubes in the trays, or pack them in bags or containers. Use this method to preserve borage flowers and the leaves of variegated mint, lemon balm or scented-leaved pelargoniums for adding to cold drinks.

Drying Dry herbs quickly to retain as much of their colour and their volatile oils as possible. They are ready for storing when crisp, but not so brittle that they crumble to dust. Store dried herbs whole or crushed in airtight, dark jars or tins in a cool place.

■ **Dry naturally** in a warm, dark and well-ventilated place, such as an airing cupboard, spare room or dry shed. For best results, spread the leaves and stems in a single layer on trays or drying racks and turn several times during the first few days. When the leaves snap easily, they are dry enough to store in airtight jars or tins, or in wooden boxes in total darkness.

■ **Tie the stems of your chosen herbs** into small bundles and suspend these from hooks or coat hangers to dry gently.

■ **To oven-dry herbs** spread them on a baking tray and place in an oven, set at a very low temperature with the door slightly open. Turn and check frequently, making sure the herbs do not get too hot.

■ **To microwave-dry herbs** first remove all stems, which sometimes spark or burn in the microwave. Spread the leaves on kitchen paper on the turntable with an eggcupful of water in the middle. Dry on full power in 30-second bursts, stirring around and testing after each session. Stop when the leaves are just dry: thyme and other small-leaved herbs take about one minute, large leaves three or four minutes. Leave in the microwave for a few more minutes to complete their drying.

■ **Allow seeds** to dry naturally for a few days, then store them in airtight jars or tins.

Infusions

Infuse the fresh taste of leafy herbs in a medium such as oil, vinegar, butter or jelly. Start by pounding the herbs to a paste in a pestle and mortar.

■ **Add the herb-pulp** to an oil (olive or sunflower), white wine vinegar or cider vinegar and allow to infuse for two to three weeks. Strain out the herbs and bottle the oil or vinegar in a clean bottle or jar with a fresh sprig of the particular herb.

■ **Blend pounded herbs** with unsalted butter and store in the refrigerator; basil, oregano and chives are all suitable.

Harvesting herb seeds

The seeds of many herbs are worth gathering for culinary use or for sowing later. Select from the largest, strongest plants if the seeds are for sowing; for culinary purposes you can gather seeds freely. Label varieties and keep them separate at all times.

■ **Harvest seeds** before they are fully ripe and shedding. As a guide, look for darkening stalks, seed heads turning yellow or brown, or a papery skin on the seed pods.

■ **Carefully cut** the stems and either dry the seed heads on trays lined with paper, or loosely bundle them inside paper bags and suspend them in a warm, airy place.

■ **Most seedheads** take two to three weeks to dry fully. Crush the pods or capsules, or shake out the dry seeds; remove as much chaff and plant material as possible.

■ **For kitchen** use, store the seeds in airtight tins or jars.

Storing seeds to sow

Keep seeds for sowing in a cool, dry place, in small labelled envelopes or used film canisters.

■ **Fresh seeds usually** germinate faster and more evenly than those kept for a year or more. Angelica seeds, for example, should be sown, either *in situ* or in small pots, within three months of gathering to avoid

Herb-flavoured oils are a wonderful way to continue enjoying your harvest, long after the fresh herbs have faded.

When the stately flowerheads of angelica turn to seed, collect and store for sowing in autumn.

disturbing the taproots later. Alternatively, keep the seeds in a refrigerator through winter, and sow direct in early spring.

■ **Seeds of many umbellifers,** such as alexanders (*Smyrnium olusatrum*), angelica, aniseed, fennel, lovage and sweet cicely (*Myrrhis odorata*), need a period of cold before they will germinate, so are best sown in autumn or late winter to take advantage of frost and low temperatures.

■ **Leave a few plants** to self-sow, such as angelica, parsley or chervil and then thin or transplant seedlings elsewhere while small. However, results may be less predictable than saving and sowing seeds yourself.

Preserving herbs

Herb	Part	Method
Basil	■ Leaves	■ Freeze; infuse in oil or vinegar
Bay	■ Leaves	■ Dry; infuse in oil or vinegar
Bergamot	■ Flowers, leaves	■ Dry
Chamomile	■ Flowers, leaves	■ Dry
Chervil	■ Leaves	■ Freeze
Chives	■ Flowers	■ Dry
	■ Leaves	■ Freeze; make butter
Coriander	■ Seeds	■ Dry
	■ Leaves	■ Freeze; make butter
Dill	■ Seeds	■ Dry
	■ Leaves	■ Freeze; infuse in vinegar
Fennel	■ Seeds	■ Dry
	■ Leaves	■ Freeze; infuse in oil or vinegar
Hyssop	■ Flowers, leaves	■ Dry; infuse in oil
Lemon balm	■ Leaves	■ Dry; freeze; infuse in oil or vinegar
Lemon verbena	■ Leaves	■ Dry; infuse in oil or vinegar
Marjoram	■ Flowers	■ Dry
	■ Leaves	■ Dry; freeze; infuse in oil or vinegar
Mint	■ Leaves	■ Dry; freeze; infuse in oil or vinegar; make jelly
Parsley	■ Leaves	■ Freeze; make butter; infuse in vinegar
Pot marigold	■ Flowers	■ Dry
Rosemary	■ Leaves	■ Dry; infuse in oil or vinegar
Sage	■ Flowers	■ Dry
	■ Leaves	■ Dry; infuse in oil or vinegar
Savory	■ Leaves	■ Dry; infuse in oil or vinegar
Tarragon	■ Leaves	■ Freeze; infuse in oil or vinegar
Thyme	■ Leaves	■ Dry; infuse in oil or vinegar

The clear crisp lines of a path and pond are slightly softened by neat mounds of herbs in the formal garden (above).
In a more informal garden, herbs mingle with other plants to create a pleasing combination of flower and foliage (left).

Creating a new herb garden

Late summer is the best time to start a new herb garden. When choosing a site, try to find the most suitable place for growing herbs and bear in mind the following points.

■ **Most herbs prefer heat** and sun, as they come from the Mediterranean. Heat concentrates their aromatic oils. Avoid planting in areas of deep shade.

■ **Shelter from cold** drying winds is vital, especially for evergreens.

■ **Good drainage is important,** so improve heavy ground with compost or leaf-mould, or make a raised bed to increase the depth of well-drained soil.

■ **Some herbs** are drought-tolerant but others prefer moist soil.

■ **Avoid frost pockets,** as damp, cold conditions can be lethal in winter, and overhanging deciduous trees can shed leaves and drip water onto plants.

■ **For convenience,** position culinary herbs as near to the kitchen as possible.

Choosing a style

Think about the herbs you would like to grow and how much space you can allocate to them. You can grow a few basic culinary varieties, such as parsley, sage, thyme, marjoram, savory and bay, in a small rectangular or circular bed up to 1.2m (4ft) wide; arrange the plants according to their heights as well as their soil requirements. A larger collection of herbs will require a little more planning.

Formal herb gardens These traditional gardens are based on symmetrical geometric shapes, such as squares, triangles or segments of a circle. Herb plants are organised in structured groups within the beds, separated by a pattern of paths in the classic potager, or divided by neatly clipped hedges in a knot garden. This kind of garden needs regular trimming to maintain its disciplined formality.

Informal herb gardens The plants in an informal herb garden are laid out in a relaxed, cottage-garden style, growing and spreading freely about the beds as they would in the wild. Although charming in appearance, this style of planting also needs careful planning and maintenance, to avoid a free-for-all of competitive, sometimes invasive plants.

Making a plan

First draw up a plan of the proposed layout on graph paper. Mark in existing features, such as paths, walls or the full spread of a tree – these may need to be incorporated into the design and could affect the final layout. Scale is important, too: it is easy to assume that you have more space than actually exists, so measure the site carefully and use the same scale when adding details like paths to your plan.

To permit easy harvesting and maintenance, make sure that the beds are no more than 1–1.2m (3–4ft) wide, unless you can include stepping stones to give you access without treading on the soil. Try to arrange for frequently used herbs to be no more than 60–75cm (2ft–2ft 6in) from a path or a stepping stone. If you are edging beds with hedges of germander, box or a similar dwarf evergreen, mark in the space that these will occupy to show how much ground is left for planting.

The role of paths
Paths divide beds into manageable units, establish the outline of a formal plan and encourage air circulation around plants, which helps to prevent disease. They need to be a realistic width, ranging from 30cm (12in) for occasional access to 1m (3ft) for main pathways where you might wish to use a wheelbarrow.

This is not wasted space because the paths can be edged with rows of chives or sweet violets, or interplanted like an alpine pavement with spreading herbs, such as pennyroyal or one of the many varieties of creeping thyme.

Constructing a herb garden

As soon as you are confident about the shape and style of your new herb garden, you can start constructing it. The best time to do this is in late summer or early autumn, when the weather is still warm enough for you to cultivate in comfort.

Preparing the ground
Thorough ground preparation is especially important when constructing a herb garden: you may need to adjust the texture or acidity of the soil, and eliminate any weeds before planting to avoid difficulties later on.

If the ground has already been cultivated, start by marking out the overall shape with pegs and string. Fork over the soil to turn in annual weeds and remove perennials, such as docks, dandelions, bindweed and creeping buttercups. Loosen any deep-

---

Plants for a herb bed

A herb bed is usually designed so that plants of similar height are gathered together in ranks, with the tallest at the back and the shortest at the front, as in a group photograph. In island beds, the tallest plants go in the centre.

Herbs for the back or centre, 1m (3ft) or more	Herbs for the middle ranks, 45cm–1m (18in–3ft)	Front rank and edging herbs, up to 45cm (18in)
Angelica	Borage	Basil
Bergamot	Bugloss	Calendula
Fennel	Caraway	Chamomile
Foxgloves	Comfrey	Chervil
Liquorice	Curry plant	Chives
Lovage	Dill	Clary
Meadowsweet	Lavender	Coriander
Mullein	Lemon balm	Cumin
Rosemary	Rue	Hyssop
Sea holly	Sage	Marjoram
Sweet cicely	Santolina	Parsley
	Tansy	Savory
	Tarragon	Sorrel
	Valerian	Thyme

Planting a box-edged herb bed

You will need
- Digging or border fork and spade
- Well-rotted garden compost
- Rake
- Trowel
- Dwarf box plants for edging
- Specimen centrepiece
- Assorted herbs for filling in

1 Dig over the soil and fork plenty of well-rotted garden compost into the top layer. Rake level and firm by tamping the soil with the rake head.

3 Find the centre of the bed by marking where diagonal lines from the corners cross, and plant the centrepiece at the same level that it was growing previously.

2 Plant dwarf box plants 8–10cm (3–4in) in from the permanent boards edging the bed. Space them about 15cm (6in) apart, round all four sides.

4 Plot the positions of the remaining herbs by standing them out in their pots at least 10cm (4in) apart. Dig holes and plant each herb firmly. If planting in dry weather, water the whole bed thoroughly afterwards.

rooted weeds first, so that you can lift them out intact, and pick out any small root fragments that might regenerate.

Uncultivated and weed-infested ground will need more extensive preparation. Fork out any perennial weeds, then double-dig the whole bed; add well-rotted manure or garden compost below the topsoil as you go. If you do this in late summer or autumn, you can leave the soil to settle over winter and then plant in spring.

Path materials It is best to construct new paths before planting, using any excavated soil to raise the level of the beds.
■ **Paving stones** are expensive but quick to lay and hard-wearing, although they need a solid, level foundation.
■ **Bricks are perhaps** the most attractive paving material, suitable for both formal and informal gardens.
■ **Coarse bark** may be laid in an 8cm (3in) layer over landscape fabric.
■ **Gravel provides** a hard-wearing surface that you can define with edging or allow to merge softly with edging plants. Although prone to weeds, gravel is ideal for planting informally with a range of small herbs.
■ **Grass is inexpensive** to lay and easy to maintain, but it is not an all-weather surface. It also requires edging, either with a hard material, such as bricks or timber boards, or with regular trimming.

A herb wheel A circular island bed of kitchen herbs is attractive and easy to make.
■ **Mark out a circle** 2–2.5m (6–8ft) in diameter. Arrange an edging of frost-resistant tiles or bricks laid flat or wedged at an angle.
■ **Divide the circle** into four or eight with straight paths of stone slabs or bricks, leaving space in the centre to plant a rosemary or bay tree.
■ **Plant up the beds** with basil, parsley, marjoram, sage, thyme, chives, chervil, rosemary and savory for a good selection.

Herb lawns Certain creeping herbs can be used as an alternative to grass for a small lawn. Traditional plants for this are corsican mint (*Mentha requienii*), *Thymus serpyllum* varieties, such as 'Goldstream' or 'Rainbow Falls', and the non-flowering chamomile, 'Treneague'. Space chamomile 10cm (4in) apart, the other herbs 20cm (8in) apart.

Before planting

- **Carry out a soil test** with a simple pH kit. If the reading is 6.5 or below, which indicates acid soil, fork a dressing of garden lime into the top 10cm (4in) of the soil. Repeat the test every two to three years.
- **Improve the drainage of clay soils** by incorporating plenty of garden compost, and add lime to the surface in autumn. The compost will aerate and open up the structure, and the lime will help to reduce stickiness. Prepare individual planting areas with plenty of sharp sand or grit. Check the drainage: if the ground stays very wet after rain, consider making a raised bed.
- **Sandy soils can be hungry** and will dry out fast in summer, so work in liberal amounts of well-rotted garden compost in areas where you will grow leaf and salad herbs. After planting apply a bark or gravel mulch to conserve moisture.

Summer is the season when all sorts of fruits ripen. Soft fruits, such as strawberries, currants and raspberries, and tree fruits, like plums, peaches and the first pears and apples, are ready for picking now. It is also time to carry out some pruning and training, and to keep plants well watered.

Summer checklist

■ **Water all kinds of fruit,** with the exception of the largest trees, and mulch to conserve moisture. Pay particular attention to recently planted fruit, those on light soils and those planted against walls.

■ **Check ties and supports** on all tree fruit. Stems swell quickly during summer, and ties may need loosening to prevent constriction.

■ **Keep the soil around** newly planted fruits free of weeds by hoeing, hand-weeding or spraying. Those planted in grass establish faster if surrounded by clear soil for the first two years.

■ **Clear up and dispose** of any fruitlets that fall prematurely, especially if they have holes or signs of damage, as these are probably victims of pest attack.

■ **Summer-prune fruits** trained as cordons, fans and espaliers, starting with red currants and gooseberries in late June, and finishing with apples at the end of July.

■ **Prune wall-trained figs** by shortening half of all new sideshoots to about six leaves and tie in to training wires those left unpruned. Rub or nip off any shoots growing towards the wall, and shorten the breastwood (shoots growing out from the wall) to three leaves.

■ **Train grape vines** by tying in new growth to training wires. On fruiting vines, pinch out shoot tips two leaves beyond a truss of flowers or fruit, and the tips of any further sideshoots after one leaf.

■ **Stop picking rhubarb** by mid July, to give plants time to recover before winter.

■ **Thin heavy sets of fruit** to prevent overcropping and reduce the risk of breaking laden branches.

■ **Protect ripening** fruit from birds and squirrels with fine-mesh netting, unless already protected by a fruit cage. This is particularly important when signs of damage appear, as raiding will continue once started.

■ **Watch for pests** and diseases and treat them at the first signs, or use appropriate deterrent measures to keep them at bay.

■ **Feed alpine** strawberries every two or three weeks with a high-potash fertiliser once they start cropping.

■ **Propagate blackberries** and hybrid berries in July by layering new canes (see above). Keep moist, and layers should be ready for transplanting in autumn.

■ **Tuck straw or mats** round strawberry plants before their ripening fruit can touch the soil.

■ **Mulch gooseberries** as a precaution against mildew.

■ **Plan new fruit plantings;** send off for nursery catalogues and explore locally available varieties. Pay particular attention to the soil, climate and pollination requirements of the new plants.

■ **Start preparing** the site where new plants are to grow.

Layering

To layer blackberries or other hybrid berries, push the tip of a cane (branch) into the soil next to the plant and peg it down using a loop of wire; make sure you strip the leaves off the cane where it makes contact with the soil. Make sure the cane stays beneath the soil and keep it moist. The layered cane should produce shoots by autumn; cut the rooted cane away from the parent plant and pot up to grow on.

When fruit trees produce a bumper crop, you may get more windfalls; gather them up if you want to avoid a surfeit of wasps too.

Fruit care

The best-quality tree fruits are the result of careful thinning and summer pruning, which aids ripening as well as next year's cropping potential. Now is also the time to clear up strawberry beds and prepare new ones.

Tree fruit Apples and, to a lesser degree, pears shed some surplus fruits in late June and early July, the so-called 'June drop'. Further thinning is usually necessary to ensure large, good quality fruit. Snip off misshapen and damaged fruits with scissors in mid June. After the June drop, thin to leave one or, at the most, two fruits in each cluster, to achieve a final spacing of about 10cm (4in) apart for dessert varieties and 15cm (6in) for culinary kinds.

■ **Thin plums in early June** to 5–8cm (2–3in) apart.

■ **Summer-prune apples** and pears trained as bushes, cordons, espaliers and fans, to keep the branch structure open and stimulate next year's fruit buds. Shorten new sideshoots growing from main branches to about five leaves, and those emerging from existing fruit spurs to one leaf; leave the growing tips at the end of branches

Using a pair of sharp secateurs, shorten the sideshoots that grow out of the main branches of trained apples and pears in mid to late July. Do not cut back the growing tips of main branches.

untouched. Prune pears in mid July and apples slightly later.

■ **Prune plums and sweet cherries** trained on walls between late June and late July. Shorten new sideshoots by a third, but leave shoots at the ends of branches unpruned. After fruiting, these pruned shoots should be further shortened to three leaves.

■ **Prune acid cherries:** 'Morello' and other culinary cherry varieties produce most of their fruit on shoots made the previous year, so pruning concentrates on encouraging a constant renewal of growth by cutting out old wood and replacing it with new. Once the tree has cropped, prune out sideshoots that have borne cherries, cutting back to a young shoot left as a replacement during

Apple and plum trees can become infested with a wide range of different moths. Pheromone traps, that can be hung among the branches of the trees, can help control these pests.

It is important to thin out clusters of apples and to take out any damaged fruits. Gently hold the apples you wish to remove and twist the stems until they come away; leave one or two in each cluster.

spring pruning. Restore weak-growing varieties that produce few new shoots, and neglected trees that only fruit on the outer fringe of the branches, by pruning out about a quarter of the old fruited wood, cutting where possible just above a young sideshoot.

■ **Prop up the heavily** laden branches of all tree fruits. Even when thinned to reduce a lavish crop of fruit, branches can be so heavily laden they may break unless supported. Ideally, prop them up with forked stakes, using pads of old blanket or sacking to protect the branch from injury, or support them with rope tied to a central stake. This is particularly important for plums, since damage can admit fungal diseases as well as spoiling the shape of the tree.

■ **Hang pheromone traps** in apple and plum trees to help to control and monitor various moth pests.

Bush fruit As crops of gooseberries and currants develop, avoid overwatering as this can cause fruit to split, but make sure the plants do not suffer from drought. Mulching the plants is a sound precaution against drying out.

When fruit trees are doing well their branches can become laden down with the crop. To avoid this weight damaging your precious trees, construct some form of support for heavier branches.

■ **Start summer-pruning** gooseberries and red or white currants in early or mid June. This opens up plants to fresh air, exposes fruit to sunlight and removes soft tips that attract aphids and mildew. Shorten all new sideshoots to about five leaves, but leave the main growing tips unpruned.

■ **Cut off gooseberry shoots** that show signs of mildew.

■ **Check gooseberries** for the small 'looper' caterpillars of sawflies. Spray with insecticide or hose off with water.

■ **Prune blackcurrants** after the last fruits are picked, or delay until winter. As the best crops are borne on young stems, encourage new growth by cutting out some of the old branches, to just above ground level or to a strong low sideshoot. Aim to remove a third of the branches each year, starting with the oldest and darkest.

■ **Watch out for reversion** of blackcurrants, indicated by a lot of coarse, narrow nettle-like leaves with fewer points on their edges than normal. This is an incurable infection, and bushes must be dug up and burned.

■ **If blackcurrant stems wilt** during August, prune them off halfway down. A dark hole in the centre of the stem is a sign of the clearwing moth; the grubs tunnel downwards so cut back stems to clean sound wood and burn the prunings.

Cane fruit Keep cane fruits under control, otherwise they can get untidy and spread where they are not wanted.

■ **Prune summer raspberry** canes as soon as the remaining fruit has been harvested. Undo the ties attaching the exhausted canes to their training wires, and cut them off at ground level. Remove weak, spindly, damaged or overcrowded new canes (distinguished by their fresh green colour) to leave four to six of the strongest. Tie these to the wires with individual twists or a continuous string looped and knotted over the wires. Space canes evenly about 10cm (4in) apart.

Autumn-fruiting raspberries grown on wires strung between fence posts must be tied in once they've reached the topmost wire.

■ **Tie in the canes** of autumn-fruiting raspberries once they reach the top wire. Space them about 10cm (4in) apart on their wires, tying them as described for pruned raspberry canes. Water well in dry weather as plants come into flower, and mulch with grass cuttings. Birds are seldom attracted to late varieties, so netting is unnecessary.

■ **Pull out raspberry** suckers growing out of line while they are small.

■ **Raspberry beetles** can be troublesome when the maggots hatch out in blackberries and hybrid berries, as well as raspberries. Treat with derris, spraying in the evening when bees are not about. Spray blackberries and hybrid berries when their flowers open, and raspberries when the first berries start to colour and again two weeks later.

■ **Bundle up the new canes** of blackberries and other hybrids to separate them from the current year's canes (see above right).

■ **Loganberries and other** hybrids need to have their old fruited canes cut out; do this also for the earliest blackberries immediately

Blackberry and hybrid berry canes

1 Tie new canes (those that will bear fruit next year) into a tall bundle; this will keep them separate from the current year's fruiting canes and help prevent wind damage.

2 Once the current year's canes have fruited, remove them at ground level using sharp secateurs. Unwrap your bundle of new canes and now tie these in place.

after harvest. Trim at ground level or just above a strong sideshoot if new growth is sparse. Tie new green canes in place, evenly arranging them on the wires according to the training system used. If your garden is very cold, bundle the new canes together for protection and tie them to the lowest wire.

Strawberries When all the fruits have been picked, remove any protective netting and shear off all the foliage and unwanted runners about 5–8cm (2–3in) above ground level; a rotary mower with the blade set high can be used for this on large beds.

■ **Remove, clean and store** protective mats from around the plants, then rake off and burn the leaves, together with any straw used for mulching. Weed between the plants.

■ **Cut off runners** unless required for new plants; alternatively, tuck them into rows of two-year-old plants to produce a heavy yield of small fruit for jam-making in the bed's third and final year.

■ **In the third year** after planting, fruit quality and size decline, so plants are usually cleared after harvest. (Some gardeners leave them for a further year to produce a large crop of small fruits for jam-making.) Fork up the plants with all their roots, shake off the soil and burn them (composting can perpetuate diseases), together with all their foliage, unused runners and any straw. Then dig over the bed and manure it, ready for planting a late crop like spring greens or a green manure.

■ **Prepare a new strawberry** bed for planting in late summer. Choose a sheltered site that is sunny or lightly shaded, where strawberries have not grown for several years. An area 1.2m (4ft) wide will accommodate two rows spaced 75cm (2ft 6in) apart. Remove all weeds, including

perennial roots, before forking in garden compost or rotted manure, at the rate of about one large bucketful a square metre or yard (strawberries prefer organic manures to artificial fertilisers). In heavy clay dig in plenty of grit or coarse compost to improve drainage. Rake the soil roughly level and leave undisturbed for a month before planting the newly rooted strawberry plants.

■ **Perpetual strawberries** will continue fruiting until the frosts. They benefit from regular watering in dry weather, together with a feed of general fertiliser in early August. As these are best grown for one or, at the most, two years, dig up the plants when cropping finishes, or pick off the oldest leaves and clear away loose debris to leave plants tidy for a second year.

Harvesting and storing

With so many fruits ripening in summer, it is worth frequent checking to see what is ready to pick. Make sure you harvest fruits regularly and while they are dry and in peak condition, preferably in the morning. This is particularly important for strawberries, but any over-ripe or rotting fruit left on a plant encourages disease. Pick fruit gently and avoid bruising it, and it will keep longer.

Strawberries These crop from late May to late July, according to variety. They ripen very quickly in hot weather, so check daily and gather all berries that are fully coloured. Pick them with the stalk, and avoid handling the berries as they bruise easily. Remove all diseased and damaged fruits.

Bush fruits Red and white currants ripen from early July, when they are shiny and with a good colour. Pick whole strings of fruit, cutting the stalks with scissors if necessary to avoid damaging the fragile fruit, and remove individual currants back in the kitchen with a table fork. You may need to go over the plants two or three times. In cool, dry weather the ripe berries will often

Straw is often laid under strawberries as a mulch; once the plants have cropped, remove the straw and burn it.

hang quite happily on bushes for several weeks without deteriorating. Blackcurrants are ready from early or mid July, when the fruits are a shiny blue-black. Either pick individual currants or wait a week or so, then harvest clusters as for red currants. Use straight away or bottle or freeze.

■ **Gooseberries need thinning** during June, so pick green fruits for cooking until well-spaced berries ripen, from early July onwards. Pick fully ripened berries carefully, as they are soft and burst easily. Crops ripen unevenly, so check over the bushes several times a week. Any gooseberries remaining in late summer will be larger, sweeter and of dessert quality, compared with the earlier varieties harvested in June and July. Their skins can be very fragile, so they need careful picking when fully ripe. Freeze or juice surplus fruits.

Cane fruits
Raspberries start to ripen in July. They are ready to pick when they are well coloured and part easily from the remains of the flower. Handle with care for they are soft and easily damaged. Late varieties such as 'Leo' continue the summer

Green gooseberries have a sharp yet aromatic flavour; cook with sugar to make desserts or turn into gooseberry jam or jelly.

season into August, often overlapping with the first autumn varieties. Check the ripening crops every two to three days and harvest all that are fully coloured and come away freely, without their stalks and plugs (autumn kinds are a little firmer and part from their plugs less readily). Bottle, freeze or preserve any surplus in syrup or alcohol.

■ **Hybrid berries** such as loganberries and tayberries ripen in mid to late summer, while the blackberry season extends from midsummer to the first frosts, according to variety. Pick, complete with plugs, when fully coloured and soft. Check for ripeness every few days, especially in warm, sunny weather. Bottle, freeze or preserve in syrup.

Cherries, peaches and plums
Sweet cherries are ripe in June. Harvest as soon as they are fully coloured, but test one or two first for flavour. Pick with the stalk, using scissors or secateurs, and use immediately.

Acid varieties ripen in August or early September. Pick when fully coloured; cut the stalks with scissors or secateurs. Bottle or freeze surplus fruits, with or without stones.

■ **The first plums ripen** towards the end of July. Test well-coloured fruits to see if they come away easily from the stalk and then check every two or three days, as crops do not ripen all together.

Plums, damsons and bullaces continue to be available until late October. Pick them when soft and fully coloured for eating immediately and for freezing (halved and

Look out for ripe red currants during July; the fruits will be ready when bright red and shiny. Use scissors to cut off whole strings of currants and then strip off indvidual fruits.

stoned). Or you can gather them slightly under-ripe for bottling and jam-making, or for keeping in a cool place for two weeks and eating fresh.

■ **Early peaches and nectarines** are ripe in July. Check if the flesh around the stalk is soft, then lift the fruit gently in the palm of your hand. If ready, it will come away easily from the stalk. Fruit ripens progressively over several weeks.

Late varieties continue ripening during August and into early September. Pick fruits when they are fully coloured and soft around the stalk, and part easily when twisted. Handle them carefully as they bruise easily. They will keep for a few days in a cool place, and surplus fruits can be bottled or frozen.

Apples and pears The earliest apples mature from late July and do not keep, and should be eaten within a week or so of picking, before the flesh becomes soft and mealy. Some mid-season varieties, which mature in late August and early September, are ripe enough to eat fresh, but others need storing first for a few weeks and will remain in good condition for another month or so.

■ **The first pears** are ready to pick during August, but need a few weeks to finish

The first early peaches will begin to be ready in July and then continue to ripen over successive weeks. Late varieties will be ready during August and September.

ripening in store, as do all later varieties. Like apples, their harvesting time is indicated by a change of colour and readiness to part easily from the tree, rather than on their readiness for eating.

■ **Apples and pears** ripen over a long period, so test before you pick by lifting one or two fruits to see if they come away without twisting or tearing; windfalls can be a good indication of ripeness. You might have to spread the harvest over several days, because fruits in the sun or on the outside of the tree often ripen first.

■ **Store only sound** fruits, and reject any with holes, insect damage, torn stalks or bruises. Spread fruits on slatted shelves, or in single layers in boxes, and make sure they do not touch each other. High-quality apples can be individually wrapped in newspaper. Or you can pack about 2kg (4–4½lb) in a clear polythene bag with the bottom corners cut off for ventilation.

■ **Store all fruit** in a cool but frost-free place with good air circulation. Check fruit every 10 days or so and remove any that are showing signs of rot.

Grapes and figs Indoor and outdoor grapes mature throughout late summer depending on their variety and the amount of heat they receive. It is best to taste to check for full ripeness, as good colour is not a reliable indication. Handling grapes removes the bloom from their skins, so harvest by cutting through the stem a short distance away on both sides of the bunch. To store for a few weeks, cut a longer section of branch so that the lower end can be inserted in a jar or bottle of water with the grapes hanging down freely. Dry surplus fruits or preserve in alcohol.

■ **Figs are ready** to pick in late summer when they are very soft and hang downwards, with fully coloured skin. Pick them carefully and eat straight away or store them in a cool place for up to a week or so. You can bottle or freeze surplus fruits.

Ordering new fruit

It is wise to order new fruit plants early to allow for the widest possible choice. Popular varieties are usually available from many outlets throughout the planting season, but unusual, rare or old-fashioned varieties, as well as recent introductions, may sell out early or be available from only specialist nurseries. Order before the end of September for satisfaction.

■ **Always buy from** a reputable source to avoid introducing diseases or poor quality plants. Where appropriate, choose certified plants: many fruits are inspected regularly to make sure they are healthy and true to type.

■ **Match fruits to the aspect** and exposure of your chosen site, and the type of soil. There are some apple varieties, for example, that thrive best in areas of high rainfall; gooseberries enjoy cool districts; raspberries dislike chalky soils; and a single red currant variety can ripen early, mid-season or late according to how warm, sunny, cool or shady is the site.

■ **Check pollination requirements.** Fruits such as blackcurrants and acid cherries are self-pollinating and will crop well in isolation. Sweet cherries, apples, pears and most plums need at least one other compatible tree with which to exchange pollen at flowering time. If you have space for only one tree, make sure it is self-fertile.

■ **Most fruit trees** are grafted, so avoid plants labelled simply 'bush' or 'standard'. The type of rootstock will decide your tree's vigour, ultimate size and start of cropping, and it is important to choose the appropriate type, identified by a name or number: a reputable garden centre or nursery will help you to make the right choice.

Preparing for planting

As soon as you have ordered your new fruit, make a start on preparing the site so that the ground has time to settle before planting in autumn. Most kinds of fruit are long-lived and, like other trees and shrubs, grow best where the soil has been thoroughly cultivated. Begin by clearing all the weeds, particularly perennial kinds; where the ground is heavily infested, cut down the top growth then spray the entire area with a weedkiller such as glyphosate.

Once the site is cleared you can cultivate and the larger the plant, the deeper the soil needs to be; strawberries will grow in shallow ground 25–30cm (10–12in) deep, whereas tree fruits need 60–75cm (2ft–2ft 6in) of well-drained soil.

■ **Double dig sites** that are poorly drained or very weedy. This can be strenuous and the work is best tackled in stages.

■ **Single digging** is sufficient for bush and cane fruits on good soil or ground that has been cultivated previously.

■ **Fruit trees** need individually prepared planting sites of about 1m (3ft) square.

■ **All soils** and sites benefit from liberal additions of garden compost or rotted manure worked in well as you dig.

■ **After cultivation** leave the ground to settle for at least six weeks. Just before planting in autumn, remove any weeds and rake in an appropriate dressing of fertiliser.

Soil improvement

When preparing a bed for new fruit trees or bushes it is well worth working some organic matter into the plot, particularly on heavy or previously uncultivated soils.

In early summer, you reap the first rewards of your labour. Early maturing herbs and vegetables must be harvested promptly to ensure they are of the highest quality when they reach the kitchen. By late summer, many plants add additional interest to the garden as they near maturity.

Apple
Malus domestica

Apples can be grown in even the smallest garden if the right rootstock is chosen and plants are trained as cordons or espaliers against a fence or wall; if grafted on a dwarfing rootstock, they will thrive in large containers. Depending on the variety, apples ripen from late summer until late autumn; later varieties often store until the following year. Early frosts can damage the blossom. Hardy.

Site Sun. Deep, humus-rich and well-drained soil.

How to grow Plant trees while dormant (spacing will depend on the rootstock chosen). Feed and mulch every spring. Prune trained trees in mid or late summer.

Artichoke, globe
Cynara scolymus

Large perennial with edible immature flowerheads. It is easy to grow but plants take up a lot of space and need to be replaced after three years. Good varieties include 'Green Globe' and 'Gros Vert de Laon'. Hardy.

Site Sun. Preferably fertile, well-drained soil.

How to grow Plant rooted offsets in early spring, 60cm (2ft) apart and 75cm (2ft 6in) between rows. Top-dress established plants with fertiliser in early spring and mulch with rotted manure or compost. While the heads are developing, water well during dry

weather. Cut the heads when they are fleshy and well formed but while the scales are still closed. After harvest cut down the old stems.

Aubergine
Solanum melongena

This has large felty leaves and purple to black or white, generally pear-shaped, fruits. Can be grown under glass or outdoors in a sheltered position. Striking as a container plant for a sunny patio. Tender.

Site Sun. Rich, well-drained soil.

How to grow Sow and grow on as for tomatoes (see page 81). Plant out 45cm (18in) apart when there is no longer a risk of frost. Alternatively, grow in pots of soil-based compost (John Innes No. 3). Pinch out growing tips when plants are

30cm (12in) high. Allow five or six fruits to set, then pinch out the branch tips. Stake large plants and feed once or twice with high-potash fertiliser when fruits are swelling. Harvest while young.

Basil

Ocimum basilicum

Bushy annual with aromatic green or purple leaves, used as an accompaniment to tomatoes in many Italian dishes and as an ingredient of pesto. Some ornamental varieties are cinnamon, aniseed or lemon flavoured. Often best in pots on a patio or windowsill. Tender.

Site Sun. Fertile, well-drained soil.

How to grow Sow seed indoors in early spring and outdoors in late spring, once all danger of frost has passed. Shelter from wind and avoid over-watering. Remove flower buds and pick leaves frequently. Grow in pots of soil-based (John Innes No. 3) or soil-less compost with added grit.

Beetroot

Beta vulgaris subsp. *vulgaris*

Easily grown edible swollen roots with deep red flesh. Choose a bolt-resistant cultivar for early sowings. Hardy.

Site Sun. Fertile and well-drained soil, not recently manured.

How to grow At the end of winter or start of spring sow seed in rows 30cm (12in) apart, under cloches that have been in place for several weeks. Thin seedlings to 10cm (4in) apart. During dry weather water thoroughly once or twice a week. Harvest as required as soon as the roots are sufficiently large.

Blackcurrant

Ribes nigrum

Blackcurrants are easy to grow and one of the richest sources of vitamin C. They need plenty of space and lavish annual feeding or manuring. 'Ben Sarek' forms a compact bush, but 'Laxton's Giant' has the largest currants. Hardy.

Site Sun, light shade. Deeply dug, rich soil.

How to grow Plant while dormant, 1.5m (5ft) apart and 10cm (4in) deeper than the previous soil level on the plant; cut down to 8cm (3in) high. Feed and mulch in spring, and water in dry weather. Prune after fruiting, cutting out a third of the old, darker stems. Harvest complete bunches of fruit when fully coloured.

Borage

Borago officinalis

Hairy-leaved annual with blue, star-shaped flowers throughout summer and autumn. Young leaves can be added to salads and dressings; the flowers are used as culinary decoration. Hardy.

Site Sun. Well-drained soil, low in fertility.

How to grow Sow seed *in situ* from spring to early autumn or in a large container of soil-less compost. Deadhead regularly to avoid over-abundant self-seeding.

Broad bean

Vicia faba

Broad beans are the earliest outdoor bean to be harvested. For overwintering early plants choose a hardy variety. Sweetly scented flowers. Hardy.

Site Sun. Fertile and well-drained soil.
How to grow For an early summer crop, sow seed in late autumn, 15–23cm (6–9in) apart with 45–60cm (18–24in) between rows, depending on height. Choose a sheltered site or protect with cloches. In early spring top-dress with fertiliser and lightly hoe into the soil. Support plants with string stretched between canes. When in flower, pinch out the young top growth to boost pod development. Pick before the pods become tough and fibrous. After harvest, cut stems almost to ground level and dig in the roots.

Broccoli (calabrese)
Brassica oleracea Italica Group

This quick-growing plant produces a large central head of tight buds, usually blue-green but sometimes purple or golden yellow. There are many varieties, all highly nutritious and well flavoured: 'Trixie' is particularly fast growing and tolerates club root disease. Not fully hardy.
Site Sun. Rich firm soil.
How to grow Sow small batches from six to eight weeks before the last frosts until early summer. Make the earliest sowings in small pots under glass and plant out 23–30cm (9–12in) apart each way when there is no longer a risk of frost; make later sowings *in situ* and thin seedlings to the planting distances given above. Water regularly and mulch to encourage fast, even growth. Cut the central head before the flower buds open and apply a high-nitrogen feed. Cut the later sideshoots when about 10cm (4in) long.

Cabbage, summer
Brassica oleracea Capitata Group

Cabbage with a compact rounded head. For an early crop sow under cover. Outdoor sowings, made when the soil is fairly warm at around 7°C (45°F), will mature from late summer onwards. Choose an early maturing variety. Hardy.

Site Sun. Alkaline, fertile, moisture-retentive soil.
How to grow In late winter or very early spring sow seed in trays under glass in gentle heat – 13°C (55°F). Prick out the seedlings into individual pots and grow on. Harden off then plant out when around 10cm (4in) high, allowing 45cm (18in) all round. Feed established plants with fertiliser. Harvest as soon as the plants are well hearted, using a knife to cut to just above soil level.

Cauliflower
Brassica oleracea Botrytis Group

Cauliflowers are grown for the white, immature flowerheads known as 'curds'. Choose a summer-maturing variety. Can be a difficult crop. Hardy.
Site Sun. Alkaline, fertile and humus-rich soil, that has been deeply dug.
How to grow Sow seed in mid-autumn in a cold frame or in midwinter under cover in gentle heat – about 13°C (55°F). Grow on young plants in individual pots in a coldframe, then harden off and plant out in early spring in a sunny, sheltered site, allowing 45cm (18in) space all around them. Keep well watered. Harvest individual curds when firm and well developed but before they open.

Cherry, sweet

Prunus avium

Grow compact cherries in bush, pyramid or fan-trained forms. A number of self-fertile varieties set a good crop. Best in a sheltered position where rainfall is light. Hardy.

Site Sun. Deep, fertile and well-drained soil.
How to grow Plant trees 3–5m (10–15ft) apart, depending on the rootstock. To avoid fruit splitting, keep the soil moist. Feed in late winter with general fertiliser and mulch with well-rotted manure or compost. Prune if necessary during the growing season. Net fruit to protect it from birds.

Chervil

Anthriscus cerefolium

Feathery foliaged annual with clusters of white flowers from spring to summer. Mild, parsley-flavoured leaves are added to salads, soups, sauces and other dishes. Hardy.
Site Partial shade. Light soil with added organic matter to improve moisture retention. Grow in pots of soil-less compost.
How to grow Sow seed *in situ* monthly from spring to early autumn.

Coriander

Coriandrum sativum

This Mediterranean annual has two distinctly different crops: the finely cut pungent leaves and the round, orange-scented seeds, an essential ingredient of many Oriental dishes. Grows best in hot, dry conditions. Tender.
Site Sun. Light, well-drained soil.
How to grow Sow seed outdoors in late spring, away from fennel plants. Do not transplant or over-water. Pick leaves frequently and support seed-bearing plants. Harvest seeds in autumn. Grow in containers of soil-less compost with added grit and extra bottom drainage.

Courgette

Cucurbita pepo

Prolific plant with either long green or rounded golden fruits. The large yellow flowers are also edible and can be cooked in batter or used as decoration. Striking as a container plant for a sunny patio. Select early maturing varieties. Tender.
Site Sun. Well-drained and fertile soil with plenty of rotted manure or compost.
How to grow In early spring sow seed under cover in gentle heat – 13°C (55°F). Place two seeds in an 8cm (3in) pot and thin later to one seedling. Grow on and plant out 1m (3ft) apart, in a sheltered site when all danger of frost is past. Keep well watered and feed with liquid fertiliser once the fruits begin to swell. Harvest regularly as soon as the fruits are large enough.

Dill

Anethum graveolens

Feathery foliaged annual with flat heads of tiny yellow-green flowers. Leaves and seeds are used to flavour soups, fish and lamb. For a regular supply of young foliage, sow successively. Hardy.
Site Sun. Well-drained soil, low in fertility.
How to grow Sow seed *in situ* in spring and early summer. Plant in pots of soil-less compost. Water during dry weather. Trim container-grown plants regularly. Dill self-seeds readily, so remove unwanted seed heads before seeds drop.

Fig

Ficus carica

A handsome, Mediterranean tree, this makes an attractive fan when trained on a warm garden or conservatory wall. Figs fruit best when the roots are confined in a large container or a pit lined with buried slabs. Not fully hardy.

Site Sun. Well-dug soil, restricted root run.
How to grow Plant in spring. Mulch heavily each spring with rotted manure or garden compost. Prune damaged and surplus branches in late spring, and shorten sideshoots in summer. Pick fruits when fully coloured and starting to split. Protect in a hard winter with layers of fleece or by wrapping branches in straw.

French bean, climbing

Phaseolus vulgaris

This tender annual is related to the dwarf french bean but is more productive and so useful where space is limited. Early sowings in a greenhouse can be harvested until outdoor beans are available and, if cut back and fed, will crop again after open-air plants are finished. Varieties with gold, purple or speckled pods, such as 'Borlotto', 'Viola Cornetti' and 'Rob Roy', make decorative features when grown on tall cane wigwams in flower borders.

Site Sun. Fertile and well-drained soil.
How to grow Sow indoors in small pots in mid-spring or outdoors from late spring until midsummer. Sow greenhouse crops in early spring. Space plants 15cm (6in) apart in rows 20cm (8in) apart or in a 1m (3ft) circle. Provide each plant with a sturdy 2.5m (8ft) cane crossed and tied in rows or as a wigwam. Keep moist, especially once flowering starts. Start picking while beans are young (eight to ten weeks after sowing) and repeat every two to three days.

French bean, dwarf

Phaseolus vulgaris

Small, bushy annual with long edible pods. Select varieties that are suitable for early sowing. Tender.
Site Sun. Fertile and well-drained soil.
How to grow In mid-spring sow seed under cover individually in small pots or modular trays. Plant out seedlings under cloches that have been warming the soil for several weeks, 10cm (4in) apart with 45cm (18in) between rows; top-dress the soil with fertiliser before planting. Keep plants well watered, especially once the flowers appear. Harvest regularly as soon as pods are sufficiently large but before the seeds are prominent.

Garlic

Allium sativum

The underground bulbs of this strongly flavoured member of the onion family keep for many months if they are ripened in the sun. Garlic produced for cultivation is more reliable than bulbs from the greengrocer, as the latter may not be suitable for cooler climates. Hardy.
Site Sun. Well-drained and fertile soil, not recently manured.
How to grow In early to midwinter plant individual cloves 10cm (4in) apart with the tip just showing, and 23cm (9in) between rows; use a trowel or dibber rather than pressing the cloves into the ground. If

drainage is poor, draw up the soil into low ridges and plant the garlic on top. Lift bulbs in mid to late summer, once the leaves have fallen over and begun to yellow. Spread in the sun to dry thoroughly.

Gooseberry

Ribes uva-crispa

The green or red berries of this prickly bush are the first soft fruits of the summer season to be picked. Usually grown as a bush but can also be trained in half-standard and cordon form. Hardy.

Site Sun. Well-drained and fertile soil, with plenty of added well-rotted manure or compost.

How to grow Plant 1.2m (4ft) apart with 1.5m (5ft) between rows. In early spring feed each bush with 50g (2oz) sulphate of potash and mulch with plenty of well-rotted manure or compost. Water well while fruit is forming but stop when it is nearly ripe, otherwise the berries may split. Fruit may need thinning from late spring onwards. Net bushes when the fruit starts to ripen to protect it from birds.

Hyssop

Hyssopus officinalis

Semi-evergreen perennial with long, narrow leaves that can be added to salads, soups, stews, stuffing and meat. Throughout summer and into early autumn it is smothered with small blue flowers. Makes an ideal low hedge or edging plant. Hardy.

Site Sun. Well-drained soil.

How to grow Sow seed in early spring in rows 30cm (1ft) apart, thin seedlings to 30cm (1ft apart). Grow in pots of soil-based compost (John Innes No. 3) with added grit. To maintain a bushy shape trim the clump in spring and again after flowering.

Lettuce

Lactuca sativa

Several different types of lettuce can be grown outdoors for cropping from early summer onwards. Choose from crispheads, like 'Webb's Wonderful'; cos types, such as 'Little Gem'; loose-leaf or 'cut-and-come-again' lettuces such as 'Lollo Rosso'; or butterhead varieties like 'Tom Thumb'. For a continuous supply, sow seeds every two to three weeks.

Site Sun. Fertile and well-drained soil.

How to grow From mid-spring onwards, sow seed in rows 23–30cm (9–12in) apart. Thin to 15–30cm (6–12in) apart, depending on the size of the variety. In cold areas or for a very early crop, sow under cover, prick out into individual pots then harden off and plant out in late spring. Keep plants well watered during dry spells. Harvest when lettuces are sufficiently large.

Loganberry

Rubus x loganbaccus

The long canes of this vigorous raspberry-blackberry hybrid make an excellent screen when trained on a fence of wires. Alternatively, grow it on a wall or training wires. Choose a thornless variety such as 'LY 654' for comfortable harvesting of the richly flavoured berries. Hardy.

Site Sun. Fertile, well-drained soil.

How to grow Plant while dormant, 3–4m (10–12ft) apart. Mulch with rotted manure or compost each spring, and water in dry weather. Tie in new canes as they develop, and prune out all the old canes after harvesting. Pick fruits when fully ripe and almost purple in colour.

Mangetout
Pisum sativum

A type of pea grown for its edible pods and seeds. Tall climbing varieties grow 1.5m (5ft) high, while smaller ones reach 75cm (2ft 6in). Varieties include 'Carouby de Maussanne', 'Oregon Sugar Pod' and 'Sugar Snap'. Tender.
Site Sun. Well-drained and fertile soil with well-rotted compost or manure dug in during winter.
How to grow Sow from early spring onwards and grow as for peas (see page 78). Harvest when the peas are just visible as tiny swellings; pick regularly to encourage the production of pods.

Marjoram
Origanum species

The three main kinds of culinary marjoram, all perennial plants that thrive in containers, are sweet marjoram (*O. majorana*), the warmer pot marjoram (*O. onites*) and pungent oregano (*O. vulgare*). The leaves aid digestion and are an ingredient of bouquet garni. Generally hardy, although sweet marjoram is slightly tender.
Site Sun. Dry, well-drained soil.
How to grow Sow seed under glass in autumn or spring. Avoid over-watering. Trim after flowering and cut back to 5cm (2in) high in late autumn. Divide or take cuttings every two years. Grow in pots of soil-based (John Innes No. 3) or soil-less compost with added grit.

Mint, apple
Mentha suaveolens

Perennial with apple-and-mint flavoured, oval-to-rounded mid-green leaves. In summer there are mauve flowers. Invasive, so grow in a large, bottomless container sunk in the ground. Hardy.

Site Sun, partial shade. Any soil except dry.
How to grow Sow seed in spring and grow in containers of soil-based compost (John Innes No. 3). Trim edges of clump regularly to limit spread.

Onion
Allium cepa

Most onions and shallots are grown from 'sets' planted in spring, but seed sown the previous year gives an early summer crop. Not fully hardy.
Site Sun. Alkaline and well-drained soil.
How to grow In late summer to early autumn, sow in rows or in blocks 30cm (12in) apart in an open, sheltered site. Thin to 5cm (2in) apart in spring and feed with general fertiliser. Harvest for eating as soon as bulbs are large enough. For storing, loosen roots with a fork when leaves flop; leave for a week, then lift and dry in sun.

Parsley
Petroselinum crispum

Dark green biennial commonly grown in two forms: the tightly curled version used for garnishing; and the more strongly flavoured French or flat-leaved variety used for both garnishing and cooking. For a year-round supply sow in spring and again in midsummer for growing under cover. Hardy.

Site Light shade in summer, but sun for winter crops. Deep, fertile soil with added compost or rotted manure.

How to grow Sow seed outdoors in spring and summer for a year-round supply. Soak seeds overnight in warm water before sowing to aid germination. Harvest regularly and remove flower stems, leaving one or two plants to self-seed if required.

Pea

Pisum sativum

Easy climbing annuals that can provide a crop in early to midsummer. Choose a suitable variety such as 'Douce Provence', 'Early Onward', 'Feltham First' or 'Kelvedon Wonder'. Hardy.

Site Sun. Well-drained and fertile soil, with well-rotted compost or manure dug in during winter.

How to grow For the earliest crops, sow in late winter under cloches, then outdoors from early spring onwards. Form a drill with a broad hoe 3cm (1¼in) deep and sow seeds 5cm (2in) apart in a triple row. Net freshly sown seed to protect from birds and put up supports such as netting or twiggy branches when the plants are 10cm (4in) high. Harvest pods when they are well filled but still young; pick regularly.

Peach

Prunus persica

These attractive trees have a froth of soft pink blossom in late spring followed by richly flavoured fruits. Best grown on a warm, sheltered wall where the blossom can be protected from frost. Dwarf plants grow 1.5m (5ft) high and are excellent for large containers. Hardy.

Site Sun. Fertile, well-drained soil.

How to grow Plant in autumn, spacing full-size trees 4m (12ft) apart. Mulch in spring with well-rotted manure and water in dry weather. Protect against frost and peach leaf curl in late winter and early spring with a sheet of polythene. Prune out surplus growth in spring, leaving a new shoot at the base of each flowering shoot. Pollinate flowers on indoor plants using a soft brush, and thin fruit clusters until fruitlets are about 10cm (4in) apart. Harvest when the fruits are soft around the stalk.

Pear

Pyrus communis

Pears need warm summers to achieve perfection and crop best if fan-trained on warm walls and sheltered from spring frost. Most need a compatible partner for cross-fertilisation. Hardy.

Site Sun. Fertile, very well-drained soil.

How to grow Plant, grow and prune pears as for apples (see page 71). Start picking from late summer, while fruits are still hard: test every week and harvest any that come away easily. Store in a cool place until fruits ripen.

Pepper

Capsicum annuum

Both large-fruited sweet peppers and slimmer hot peppers, or chillies, grow on sun and heat-loving bushy plants. Where summers are cool, peppers are best grown under glass or on a warm patio sheltered from cool winds. Tender.

Site Sun. Rich, well-drained soil.

How to grow Sow in late winter as for tomatoes (see page 81) or buy young plants in late spring. Pot up seedlings into 8cm (3in) pots of soil-based compost (John Innes No. 3), moving them into larger ones as they grow. Harden off outdoor plants and plant out 45cm (18in) apart when there is no longer a risk of frost. Pinch out growing tips when 38cm (15in) high. Water regularly during flowering and fruiting, and feed every 10–14 days. Harvest sweet peppers green or fully coloured; let chillies ripen and then dry on strings for two weeks before storing.

Plum

Prunus domestica

Plums, gages and damsons are all vigorous trees, even when grafted on a semi-dwarfing rootstock, and are best trained on a wall as fans or left to make large specimen trees, sheltered from cold spring winds. A few varieties, such as 'Victoria', are self-fertile but most need a pollen partner. Dessert, cooking and dual-purpose varieties are available. Hardy.

Site Sun. Rich, deep moist soil.

How to grow Plant in late autumn, spacing bushes 2.5m (8ft) apart and other kinds 4.5m (15ft) apart. Mulch generously each

spring with rotted manure. Thin fruits in early summer and support heavily laden branches to prevent them breaking. Only prune trees in leaf, removing misplaced shoots and some that have carried fruit. Harvest ripe fruits, checking every two to three days, and use immediately.

Potato, first early

Solanum tuberosum

These edible tubers are classified according to when they mature, with 'first earlies' maturing in early to midsummer. They can be grown outside with protection or if 'earthed up' with soil. They are ready when the flowers are fully open, around three months after planting. Not fully hardy.

Site Sun. Acid, fertile and well-drained soil, deeply dug.

How to grow Set seed potatoes to sprout, or 'chit', at the end of winter and plant out in early spring, 15cm (6in) deep with 30cm (12in) between tubers and 60cm (2ft) between rows. Before planting, rake in a general fertiliser. Protect with fleece or polythene, or mound the soil over the rows every two to three weeks. During dry weather, water well once a week. Use a fork to lift carefully as needed.

Potato, second early

Solanum tuberosum

Ready two to three weeks after 'first earlies', varieties like 'Catriona', 'Marfona' and the salad type 'Belle de Fontenay' give slightly heavier yields of 'new' potatoes or can be left until larger and dug up for storing. Not fully hardy.

Site Sun. Deeply dug fertile and well-drained soil.

How to grow Sprout tubers in late winter, as for first earlies, and plant in mid-spring 10–15cm (4–6in) deep and 38cm (15in) apart each way. Water and mound soil halfway up the stems every two to three weeks. Start lifting tubers with a fork when flowers are fully open.

Raspberry
Rubus idaeus

Summer-fruiting raspberries crop at different times depending on the variety. They thrive in sun in cool climates but prefer partial shade in hot areas. Hardy.
Site Sun, partial shade. Fertile and well-drained soil, slightly acid and with plenty of added well-rotted manure or compost.
How to grow Grow on a framework of 1.5m (5ft) high posts and horizontal wires, 30cm (12in) apart. Plant dormant canes in autumn or early winter 40cm (16in) apart, with the topmost roots no more than 5cm (2in) below the surface of the soil, and cut back to 15cm (6in) high. In spring, feed with general fertiliser and mulch generously with well-rotted manure or compost. Water well in dry weather but not while the fruit is ripening. After harvest, cut old canes at ground level and tie in new ones 10cm (4in) apart, fanning them out if necessary.

Red and white currants
Ribes sativum

Easy and reliable. Grown as bushes, half standards or cordons in warm, sheltered sites. Hardy.
Site Sun. Fertile and well-drained soil, preferably slightly acid and with plenty of added compost or well-rotted manure.
How to grow Plant 1.2m (4ft) apart with 1.5m (5ft) between rows. In early spring feed each bush with 50g (2oz) per bush of

sulphate of potash and mulch with well-rotted manure or compost. In summer, pull off suckers produced from below ground.

Runner bean
Phaseolus coccineus

A popular tender perennial, usually grown as a half-hardy annual, with lush foliage and decorative scarlet, white, pink or bicoloured flowers. Most varieties are climbers, but a few, such as 'Gulliver' and 'Pickwick', are naturally dwarf, and all can be grown as 45cm (18in) high plants by pinching out growing tips regularly. Train on sunflowers to make a feature. Tender.

Site Sun, light shade, sheltered from strong winds. Deep, moist and fertile soil.
How to grow Sow as for climbing beans (see page 75), and plant out after the last frosts, 15cm (6in) apart in rows or circles. Water freely in dry weather, especially during flowering, and mulch. Start harvesting before the seeds are visible through the pods, and pick every few days until the autumn frosts.

Strawberry
Fragaria x *ananassa*

Strawberry plants crop well for several years and different varieties provide a succession of fruit throughout summer. Hardy.

Site Sun. Fertile and well-drained soil, preferably slightly acid and with plenty of well-rotted manure.

How to grow Plant in autumn or early spring in deeply dug, well-manured ground, containers or raised beds. Use soil-based compost (John Innes No. 3) if you plant in pots. Space 30–38cm (12–15in) apart with 1m (3ft) between rows. In late winter feed with sulphate of potash. Feed older plants with a general fertiliser if their vigour declines. After flowering, water thoroughly every two weeks in dry conditions. Net to protect the fruit from birds.

Strawberry, alpine

Fragaria vesca

This compact perennial bears flushes of small, intensely fragrant red, yellow or white berries from midsummer until the autumn frosts. The berries are usually overlooked by birds, so rarely need netting. Excellent for edging and containers, and as ground cover under fruit trees. Hardy.

Site Sun, light shade. Well-dug, fertile soil.

How to grow Buy young plants or sow seeds in warmth or outdoors from early spring onwards. Plant out in late spring, about 30cm (12in) apart. Feed each spring and mulch with compost or grass clippings. Water fruiting plants regularly. Harvest fruit when fully coloured and soft. Divide and replant every three to four years.

Sweetcorn

Zea mays

A superb crop for home-growing because the flavour and sweetness of the cobs start to deteriorate minutes after picking. The tall plants are decorative and sturdy enough to support climbing beans (see page 75) planted at their base. In cool gardens, choose early-ripening varieties. Tender.

Site Sun. Rich, firm well-drained soil.

How to grow Sow seeds individually in small pots in a warm place indoors, about six weeks before the last frosts occur.

Harden off outdoors and plant out 35cm (14in) apart each way in blocks. Water well when flowers appear and again when cobs are swelling. Harvest cobs when their tassels turn brown and the kernel contents are milky. Use immediately.

Tomato

Lycopersicon esculentum

For the best flavour, tomatoes should be grown outdoors, sheltered from cool winds, but where summers are cool they are an ideal crop for greenhouse borders, containers or growing bags. The most productive kinds are tall varieties, grown on canes or strings as single stems; naturally bushy varieties crop earlier and make decorative pot or hanging basket plants. There is a huge choice available, including red, yellow, green or striped fruits in a range of sizes, from small 'cherries' to enormous 'beefsteak' varieties for slicing. Tender.

Site Sun. Fertile, well-drained soil with plenty of humus.

How to grow Sow indoor crops between midwinter and early spring according to the amount of heat you can provide; sow outdoor varieties eight weeks before the last frosts. Germinate seed at 15°C (59°F) and prick out seedlings into small pots. Plant out when the first flower truss is visible, after hardening off. Train tall varieties on supports, removing sideshoots; leave bush types unpruned. Water regularly and feed every 10–14 days after flowering starts. Harvest fruits when fully coloured.

Autumn

As many vegetables approach maturity during autumn, it is now time to harvest and store your precious produce before the first frosts strike. Start planning for next year's crop as you clear the ground: thorough preparation now will improve plant growth and increase yields in the future.

Maincrop carrots can be harvested in autumn and stored for later use. Clean off the soil and keep in boxes layered with damp sand.

Autumn checklist

■ **Check crops regularly and harvest** when ready. Freeze excess produce where this method suits or store in a cool, dry room.

■ **After harvest, clear away** plants that have cropped. Put any green waste or crop remnants onto the compost heap unless it has been affected by pests and disease, in which case it should be burned or disposed of in a dustbin.

■ **Dig over and manure** the soil in your vegetable plot as soon as it is cleared of crops. This is particularly important on heavy soils, which will benefit from being broken down by winter frosts. By leaving the soil in ridges it will also keep drier through the winter.

■ **Plan and prepare for the next year,** once the ground is clear and cultivated. Then you can start off next year's crops, or leave the soil vacant so the frost can help to improve its structure.

■ **Earth up any hardy brassicas** to prevent wind rock over winter.

■ **Remove the supports** used for any climbing crops and detach the remnants of the spent plants. Then sort and bundle the supports and store somewhere dry until the following year.

■ **Continue to hoe** the vegetable plot regularly to ensure you kill weed seedlings as they emerge.

■ **Remove and burn** the stems of maincrop potatoes if they are affected by potato blight.

Several members of the cabbage family can be sown in autumn; protect seedlings against attack by birds with netting.

Crops in autumn

Autumn is the ideal time to clean up the vegetable garden and make a fresh start for next year. As the various crops come to the end of their productive cycles, dispose of their debris as you harvest, rather than leaving the remnants *in situ* where they could harbour pests and diseases. This also leaves the soil clear for digging. Remember to burn any plant material that has been infected with disease.

Peas and beans There should still be plenty of legumes ready to harvest in autumn. Continue to harvest peas, french beans and runner beans as they become ready. Freeze any glut and consider leaving some for drying.

■ **Sow broad beans** and early peas for cropping next spring to summer.

■ **Sow early cultivars of peas** under cloches to be ready for picking in early summer. The cloches will be essential for winter protection after the seedlings have emerged.

■ **Sow broad beans** to harvest from late spring to early summer. Longpod cultivars are the hardiest.

■ **Harvest maincrop peas** for using fresh when the seeds have swollen and the pods are still green. Removing pods will encourage flowering and, therefore, a further yield of peas.

Sowing early peas and beans

1 Sow peas in a block after taking out a spade-width of soil. Sow in three rows, staggering the spacing. Cover with cloches.

2 Sow broad beans 15cm (6in) apart in rows 60cm (2ft) apart, to overwinter and crop in summer.

3 On exposed sites, protect the young broad bean plants with a layer of fleece, or grow them under cloches.

Harvesting now

Autumn is a time when many vegetables yield their crops. The following are ready to harvest:

- Beetroot
- Carrots
- Celeriac
- Celery
- Chinese cabbage
- Florence fennel
- French and runner beans
- Jerusalem artichokes
- Kale
- Leeks
- Lettuces and salad leaves
- Maincrop potatoes
- Marrow
- Onions
- Parsnips
- Peas
- Pumpkins and squash
- Salad radish
- Salsify
- Scorzonera
- Spinach and spinach beet
- Spring onions
- Summer and autumn cauliflowers
- Summer, autumn and winter cabbages
- Swedes
- Turnips

■ **For dried peas and beans** cut the plants off at ground level when the seeds are visibly swollen. Allow the vines to remain hanging on the support to dry out before harvesting the pods.

TIP Leave the roots of peas and beans in the ground after the last crop has finished: they contain high levels of nitrogen, which will benefit a follow-on crop of brassicas.

Cabbage family As far as brassicas are concerned, some jobs need doing at the start of autumn, while others are better left until the end of the season.

■ **Use up summer and autumn** cabbages. In early autumn, harvest these less hardy crops that will not store for long periods before you consider cutting the hardier winter cabbages.

■ **Transplant spring cabbages** into their cropping site in early autumn. Space the young cabbages 30cm (12in) apart in rows 30cm (12in) apart. After planting, tug one of the leaves; the cabbage seedling should remain firmly bedded in the soil. If it moves, plant the seedling again more firmly.

■ **In order to achieve a succession** of spring cabbages, sow more seed under cloches ready to transplant in early spring. Where headed cabbages and loose-leaved spring greens are both required, plant the cabbages closer together in the rows. Then remove alternate plants to eat as spring greens and leave the others to form a head.

■ **Sow summer cauliflowers** in early autumn under the protection of a cloche or in modular trays in a coldframe.

■ **Earth up the soil** around the stems of cabbages, cauliflowers and brussels sprouts early in the season; this helps to prevent them from rocking in later winds and loosening their roots in wet soil conditions.

■ **Sow turnips** in early autumn for a leafy crop of greens, or turnip tops, but choose a hardy variety such as 'Green Stone Top'.

■ **In September or October,** transplant chinese cabbage and chinese broccoli sown in trays in late summer. Plant them out under the protection of cloches or low polythene tunnels.

■ **Sow texsel greens** (*Brassica carinata*) in early autumn under similar protection as a

Some winter cabbages can be harvested now: cut and store in a frost-free but unheated place with good air circulation.

cut-and-come-again crop for late autumn and early winter. Keep sowings well watered to ensure swift germination and rapid early growth. Cut the leaves in five to six weeks when they are about 25cm (10in) high.

■ **During late autumn,** cut winter cabbages of the Dutch winter-white type. They can be stored in a cool, frost-free place with good air circulation for up to three weeks.

■ **Harvest savoy** and 'January King' cabbages as required. These are hardy enough to stand over winter in the garden.

■ **Protect spring cabbages** with cloches or fleece when long periods of frost are forecast in late autumn.

■ **Cover chinese cabbages** with low polythene tunnels, cloches or fleece during cold weather as they can only withstand very light frost.

■ **Protect cauliflowers** by drawing up the outer leaves and tying them to cover the curd when frosty weather is forecast. It is the rapid thaw on mild sunny days that damages the curd rather than the cold weather itself.

Onion family Finish lifting bulb onions as soon as is possible. Dig them up and leave them lying on the ground or place them in trays to allow the skins to cure in the sun, but bring them inside if persistent rain threatens and before the first frost.

■ **Store the onions** after the tops have died and dried off. Clean off any soil and all withered roots, twist off the old dead leaves and hang in strings or nets, or simply place on open trays in a cool, airy and frost-free place.

TIP In a wet season, if the onion tops are slow to die down, bend the leaves over just above the swollen part, or neck. This speeds the process of dying down.

If your soil is heavy, create a ridge of soil and plant garlic cloves along the top; this will aid drainage.

■ **Plant garlic cloves** now, as they need at least two months of cold weather in order to grow well, and a longer growing season produces larger bulbs the following year.

■ **Plant sets (small bulbs)** of the hardier types of onion, but only if your soil is light and free draining.

■ **Harvest leeks** with a garden fork as you need them; they are hardy enough to stand through the coldest winter months.

Potatoes and root crops There are various ways in which you can extend the harvest of your root crops. Many can be stored in or out of the ground to last through the coming months and still taste good. The method you choose will depend on the amount of excess produce you have and how long you wish to store it.

■ **Cover carrots and parsnips** in the row with loose straw, after the foliage has died down. In this way you can store them in the ground over winter, but keep a watch for mice that might hide in the straw and eat the roots.

■ **Harvest maincrop carrots** and wash off the dirt. Cut off the feathery tops. Fill a box with a layer of damp sand and lay a single layer of carrots on top. Cover the carrots with a further layer of sand. Continue filling the box with alternating layers of sand and carrots. Store the box or boxes in a cool, frost-free shed.

■ **Earth up florence** fennel once the stem bases begin to swell and protect plants with cloches to extend the harvesting season.

■ **Dig up beetroot** as soon as the foliage starts to die down and store in a clamp (see page 88) or box of moist sand.

■ **Lift maincrop** potatoes as the foliage dies down. If possible, leave the tubers on the soil surface for a few hours to allow the skins to harden.

■ **Store large quantities** of potatoes in a clamp outdoors (see below). The straw and soil casing will insulate the tubers and protect them from frost.

■ **Lift salsify and store** in boxes of damp sand in a cool shed as for carrots.

■ **Lift and store turnips** in clamps (see below), or cover them in the row with loose straw where they will keep until Christmas.

■ **Cover scorzonera** roots in the row with loose straw and lift as required.

Perennial crops Autumn is the time to tidy up some perennial crops as their growing season comes to an end.

■ **Cut asparagus** stalks down to ground level, and burn.

■ **Prune jerusalem** artichoke stems to the ground and compost, or cut and lay them over the row of tubers as winter protection and to make lifting easier in frosty weather.

Salads and tender crops Make the most of the last warm days and harvest any remaining salads and more tender crops.

■ **Cut down tomato plants** and hang them in a cool dry shed or greenhouse to allow the remaining fruits to ripen.

■ **Harvest pumpkins and squash** and leave them outdoors to ripen their skins.

A cloche or coldframe will offer enough protection to grow winter lettuce in a bed outdoors; open to allow ventilation on warm days.

■ **Sow seeds of winter lettuce** and winter spinach under fleece or cloches at 14-day intervals to ensure a continuity of crop.

■ **Cover spinach plants** with cloches or a polythene tunnel to extend the harvesting season into early winter.

■ **Cut and harvest marrows** before the first frosts. They will store for several months laid on open trays in a cool, frost-free place with a good flow of air.

■ **Leave dead** sweetcorn stems in place on exposed sites to provide some wind protection for those crops that remain.

Building a clamp

A clamp is a protective casing in which to store potatoes and other root crops outdoors during inclement weather. It is important to choose a well-drained site for a clamp, or the potatoes, or other roots, may become waterlogged and rot. Choose a north-facing position, so that the clamp has a cool, even temperature, which encourages the tubers to stay in good condition.

■ Spread straw over the soil, about 20cm (8in) thick, and pile the potatoes on this base.

■ Cover the tubers thickly with more straw and top this with a 10cm (4in) layer of soil, taken from around the clamp to leave a drainage 'moat'.

■ Pull some wisps of straw through the top to make a ventilation chimney, then pat firm the earthen sides with the back of a spade.

■ Other roots like beetroots, carrots, celeriac and turnips can also be stored in a clamp after you have removed any leafy tops.

Although many herbs are still providing useful pickings for the kitchen, the emphasis is now on clearing and tidying the herb garden. Many perennials can be planted out now and you can pot up herbs for winter use; make sure the specimens you choose are healthy and growing strongly.

Autumn checklist

■ **Continue harvesting** the leaves of basil, mint and rosemary, and the stems or roots of horseradish, liquorice and orris for immediate use or storage.

■ **Pot up selected herbs,** including self-sown parsley, early in the season for winter use. Later on, bring a batch indoors for growing on a windowsill.

■ **Extend the picking** season of outdoor herbs, such as parsley, as temperatures fall, by covering them with cloches or fleece.

■ **Insulate potted herbs** outdoors or bring them under cover if frost threatens. Before the first frost, move under glass tender herbs such as lemon verbena, pineapple sage and french lavender.

■ **Scorch any beds of mint** that are affected by rust with a flame gun or a small fire of straw and kindling, to kill the spores and sterilise the soil.

■ **Dig the site** for a new herb garden and leave rough over winter for spring planting.

■ **Start planting** hardy perennials such as mint and comfrey.

■ **Make final sowings** of chervil and lamb's lettuce in a coldframe, spent growing bag or cool greenhouse border.

■ **Lift and divide** large clumps of perennial herbs such as fennel, tarragon, lemon balm and lovage.

■ **Plant evergreen herbs,** such as box, curry plant or lavender, as edging for beds and borders on light soils and in mild gardens; elsewhere, especially on heavy or cold ground, planting is best done in April or late summer.

■ **Check any layers** of thyme and rosemary pegged down in early summer as well as leggy plants 'dropped' in spring or winter, and separate the young plants if they have

Leave the flowerheads of herbs such as angelica on the plant to form attractive seedheads.

rooted. If not, re-peg the layers and look again in early spring.

■ **Continue clearing away** old growth and spent flowerheads, but leave some of the more decorative specimens as food for foraging birds. Top-dress bare soil with garden compost.

■ **Take hardwood cuttings** of elderberries to root outdoors. Once rooted, plant them out as the traditional guardians of herbs and herb gardens.

■ **Cut back chives** as the leaves turn brown and start to die down.

■ **Sow the seed of umbellifers,** such as angelica, caraway and lovage, in a coldframe or greenhouse.

■ **Gather seed heads** to dry for kitchen use or to sow in spring.

Potting up winter supplies

If you have not already potted up plants of basil, chives, parsley, small tarragons, marjoram and mint from the garden for winter use, do so as soon as you can.

■ **Divide large clumps of herbs** and pot them up into individual containers.

■ **Keep the pots in the greenhouse** or in a lightly shaded place outdoors, sheltered from cold winds, and water them if necessary.

■ **Before moving plants indoors,** check carefully for signs of aphids or other pests; a precautionary spray of insecticidal soap will help to control pest numbers.

■ **Augment herb supplies** by exploring garden centres for end-of-season bargains. Young plants of thyme, sage, rosemary and salad burnet are a good size for growing on windowsills indoors, before planting out in the herb garden next spring.

Dividing herbs

Every three to four years, lift and divide vigorous clump-forming herbs to control and rejuvenate their growth. Do this early in autumn in mild, protected areas, otherwise wait until March or April. Ideal herbs to divide include, fennel, lovage, tarragon and lemon balm.

■ **Cut back old top growth** close to the ground, then ease out the clump by inserting a fork all round the outside and levering the plant upwards.

■ **Use a spade to chop the clump up** into smaller segments. You may find it easier to split very large clumps *in situ* and then fork up the segments.

■ **Replant only the young** outer sections in fresh soil, then firm. Water in dry weather.

Planting hardy herbs

Plant new perennial herbs in September, while the soil is still relatively warm. Water the plants and allow them to drain before planting them in prepared sites; large plants can be cut into two or more portions using a sharp knife.

Horseradish is grown for the fiery pungent flavour of its roots; the longer the roots stay in the ground, the hotter they are.

■ **Dig a hole large** enough to accommodate the roots of your herbs comfortably. Fork over the soil in the bottom and mix in a little potting compost.

■ **Loosen any tightly** wound roots before planting. Make sure that the top of the rootball is at surface level and replace the excavated soil.

■ **Firm gently** and water well if conditions are dry.

Harvesting and drying roots

The small roots of arnica, angelica, liquorice and marshmallow can be dried whole. Plants with larger roots, such as dandelions, horseradish, lovage, orris and sweet cicely, are better split lengthways and then sliced before drying.

■ **Dig up roots when growth** has ceased and plants are dormant. Lift them carefully with a spade or fork to avoid damage, wash off the soil, remove any top growth and cut off thin, fibrous roots.

■ **Dry the roots in a microwave** on full power in 30-second bursts.

■ **Alternatively, dry them in** a conventional oven set at 50ºC (120ºF), until they are light and fragile. Allow the roots to cool, then store them in airtight tins.

As the harvest draws to a close for another year, it is time to start tidying up and planting new fruit while conditions outdoors are still clement. Peaches and cane fruits need pruning, and it is worth taking some hardwood cuttings of bush fruits like gooseberries and currants.

Autumn checklist

■ **Harvest fruit as soon as it ripens.** Gather everything by the end of October or just before the first frosts are forecast, and carefully store those varieties that keep well. Check fruit in store regularly.

■ **Order new fruit** soon for autumn and early winter planting, if you haven't done so already, and before all the choice varieties are sold out.

■ **Take measures to combat** peach leaf curl if it has been a problem in previous seasons (see page 93).

■ **Finish preparing** the ground for new fruit (see page 97); clear away weeds, dig over the planting sites and work plenty of garden compost or well rotted manure into the soil. Dig in any green manures that were sown on the plot after strawberries were lifted in early summer.

■ **A month after preparing** a new plot, plant out the new fruit trees or bushes if the soil is in a workable condition.

■ **If you can't plant immediately,** protect new bare-rooted fruit plants by 'heeling' them into a spare piece of ground.

Pick apples and pears when they are ripe. Store varieties that keep well and turn others into sauces, juice or chutneys.

■ **Prune fan-trained** peaches before the end of September.

■ **Take hardwood cuttings** of healthy bush fruits and root them in open ground.

■ **Protect fruit trees** from attacks by winter moths by fixing grease bands around their trunks in October.

■ **Pot up strawberries** in 13cm (5in) pots for early fruiting under glass. Stand them outside until late November, then bring under glass.

■ **Dig up and divide** rhubarb for replanting in fresh ground, but leave this until the spring on heavy soils.

■ **Start winter pruning** apples and pears in November when crops have been picked and leaves have fallen.

■ **Remove the roof netting** from your fruit cages. This allows birds to get into the cages and clear up many of the pests remaining on plants or hibernating at ground level. It will also reduce the risk of heavy snow damaging the netting.

Harvesting now

Autumn is a time when may fruits ripen. The following are ready to harvest:

■ Apples	■ Pears
■ Apricots	■ Plums
■ Blackberries	■ Quince
■ Blackcurrants	■ Raspberries
■ Figs	■ Alpine
■ Grapes	strawberries
■ Medlars	■ Perpetual
■ Nectarines	strawberries
■ Peaches	

Storage times

Late apples

'Ashmead's Kernel'*	December–March
'Blenheim Orange'	November–January
'Bramley's Seedling'*	November–March
'Crispin' (syn. 'Mutsu')	November–February
'Golden Noble'*	October–January
'Howgate Wonder'*	November–February
'Orleans Reinette'	December–February
'Ribston Pippin'	November–January
'Spartan'	November–January
'Sturmer Pippin'	December–April
'Sunset'	November–December
'Suntan'	December–March

Pears

'Catillac'*	December–April
'Joséphine de Malines'	December–January
'Packham's Triumph'	November–December
'Winter Nelis'	November–January

* cooking varieties

Storing apples and pears

Although, ideally, apples and pears are left on the tree until they are ripe enough to pick easily, late-maturing varieties are best cleared by the end of October or early November, and stored. This applies particularly to pears such as 'Docteur Jules Guyot' and 'Beurre Hardy', which should be brought indoors to continue ripening before the weather deteriorates.

■ **For long storage,** keep apples and pears in an airy, cool but frost-free place.

■ **Pears benefit** from slightly warmer conditions than apples, and ripen best at about 10°C (50°F). As pears spoil quickly, check them every two or three days to see if they are ready to eat by gently pressing the stalk end for signs of softening.

■ **Wrap individual fruits** loosely in a sheet of newspaper and arrange in a single layer in a shallow wooden or cardboard box.

■ **Alternatively, store apples** in plastic bags, pierced to allow in some air. Keep no more than three to a bag.

■ **Inspect all stored fruit** regularly. Remove any that show signs of damage or disease and use immediately or discard.

Fruit-tree problems

Trap winter moths by fixing grease bands round the trunks of apple, pear, plum and cherry trees. If left untreated these insects will cause extensive damage to the leaves, blossom and shoots. A barrier of insecticidal grease applied in October will trap the wingless female moths as they emerge late in autumn and winter and climb the tree to lay their eggs.

■ **Spread the insecticidal grease** onto a strip of paper, 10cm (4in) wide, fixed to form a continuous band around the trunk; prepared grease bands are also available. Alternatively, spread the grease directly onto the bark of the tree.

Bitter pit

Bitter pit is a disorder of apples that renders the fruit inedible. It is the result of calcium deficiency, which causes dark sunken pits on the skin and brown bitter spots within the flesh, especially on the fruit of young trees. Most apple trees outgrow the problem, but useful preventative measures include watering regularly and mulching in dry weather. If a soil test shows the pH is lower than 6.5, lime around the tree.

Rake up any windfalls that can't be used for eating and burn or thoroughly compost to destroy pests and disease spores.

■ **Tree stakes** provide an alternative route for the moths, so grease these too.
■ **Check occasionally** that the bands are still sticky, and leave in place until April.
■ **Rake up any fallen fruit** that is too damaged to harvest for eating. If you leave rotting fruit lying beneath fruit trees it can encourage pests and diseases.

Autumn fruit care

Cane fruits and trained peaches will need pruning in autumn, while bush fruit and rhubarb can be propagated now.

Rhubarb Although rhubarb is perennial and seems to thrive even when neglected, it does benefit from regular division and replanting in fresh soil once every four or five years. If your soil is light, divide rhubarb crowns in late autumn, but wait until the following spring if you garden on heavy ground.
■ **Dig up a complete** crown and cut it vertically with a spade into segments, each with

Use a spade to dig up and divide rhubarb crowns. Cut the crown up so that there are two or three dormant buds on each segment.

two or three fat dormant buds at the top. Alternatively, use a spade to split the crown where it is growing and then lift each division separately.
■ **Discard the old central** portion of the crown as well as any rotten pieces.
■ **Replant the healthy** outer portions about 1–1.2m (3–4ft) apart, in soil that has been deeply dug and enriched with plenty of rotted manure.
■ **Leave any surplus segments** exposed on the surface for six to eight weeks. Then you can force them in the greenhouse for an extra early crop.

Peaches Protect late varieties, such as 'Bellegarde', which may not finish cropping before the first frosts. If low temperatures are forecast, cover unharvested fruit with fine netting or fleece, which will also help to deter birds.
■ **Prune fan-trained** trees as soon as cropping ends by cutting out the fruited sideshoots back to young low shoots, and tie these in as replacements. Also cut out any dead, broken or old exhausted branches. To avoid future disease problems, complete this pruning by the end of September and protect all cuts with wound paint.
■ **If peach leaf curl** has been a problem in previous seasons, take steps to prevent its recurrence by spraying trees with copper fungicide just as the leaves are about to fall. Gather up the leaves and burn them. Protecting plants with a polythene screen during winter is a further precaution.

Cane fruits Cut back the fruited canes of summer raspberries to ground level, if you haven't done this earlier, and tie in the new canes as replacements. Trim very tall canes to 15cm (6in) above the

Training autumn-fruited raspberries onto wires makes the plants easier to prune and the fruits easier to harvest.

top training wire, or bend the tops down and tie them to the wire.

■ **Continue harvesting** autumn raspberries until frost finishes the crop. You can cover the plants with a layer or two of fleece on cold nights to help to extend the harvest for a week or two.

■ **Prune blackberries** and hybrid berries by cutting out those canes that have fruited at ground level. In mild areas, fan out the young, replacement canes and tie these to the wires.

■ **In colder gardens,** bundle the young canes of blackberries and hybrids together and tie them on the lowest wire; fan them out in spring.

■ **Sever rooted tip** layers of blackberry and hybrid berries taken in summer, and transplant them into their growing positions.

Bush fruit Take hardwood cuttings from gooseberry and currant bushes as soon as the leaves have fallen. The cuttings root slowly and should be left undisturbed until next autumn, when they can be moved to their final positions.

Strawberries You can still plant summer-fruiting strawberries. However, with only a short time to get established these plants will not crop well in their first summer and it is usual to remove their first flush of flowers next spring to help the plants to build up strength.

■ **Larger pot-grown** strawberry plants and cold-stored runners (often sold as '60-day' or '80-day' plants) will produce a small crop of fruit next summer but should not be forced during their first year.

■ **If the autumn is dry,** continue watering summer-planted strawberries regularly until there is substantial rainfall.

■ **Perpetual strawberries** often continue fruiting until the first frosts, or a little after if you protect plants with cloches or fleece. Do not cut plants down after fruiting, but simply

Peach leaf curl causes peach leaves to become distorted and blistered, then covered with a white bloom before falling from the tree.

tidy them by removing all mulching material and weeds, and lightly fork over the soil between plants. Transplant runners to a new bed and these will give a full crop next year.

Bare-rooted plants To give new fruit plants the best start you should plant them early in the dormant season, in well-prepared ground that is not frozen or waterlogged. Plant bare-rooted trees and bushes as soon as they are delivered (see page 98); if soil or weather conditions are unsuitable, make sure the roots are kept covered to prevent them from drying out. Well-packed plants will be safe for several days if stored undisturbed in a cool, frost-free place.

Where the delay is likely to be longer, 'heel in' the trees or bushes in a spare piece of ground in a sheltered part of the garden.

■ **Dig a shallow trench** large enough to take the roots. Unpack the plants soon after delivery and lay them in the trench at a shallow angle so that they are safe from wind damage; cover the roots with soil excavated from the trench.

■ **Alternatively, gather the plants** into a sheltered corner and heap damp straw or autumn leaves over their roots.

Taking cuttings of bush fruit

1 Select strong, straight stems of this year's growth on healthy plants. Cut the base just below a leaf joint and remove the thin growing tip to leave a cutting about 30cm (12in) long. For gooseberries and red and white currants, rub off all but the top four or five buds. For blackcurrants, leave all buds intact.

2 Dig a long slit trench with a spade in a sheltered area of weed-free ground. Push in the cuttings about 10cm (4in) deep and 15cm (6in) apart, and firm with your foot. On heavy soil, cover the bottom of the slit with 5cm (2in) of sharp sand before inserting the cuttings.

Figs need plenty of warmth to produce a good crop of ripe fruit; grown against a wall, they benefit from the reflected heat of the sun.

Creating a fruit garden

Fruit can be grown in a smaller space than you might imagine possible, but to ensure regular and high-quality crops, you need to select a site that satisfies the requirements of the chosen plant.

Assessing the site Local climate is probably the strongest influence on what type of fruit you can grow. Although you can relieve the effects of high rainfall with efficient drainage, and compensate for too little rain by improving the soil and watering, other factors will be critical to the productivity of your fruiting plants.

■ **The temperatures experienced** in your garden play an important role. Fruits such as peaches, apricots and figs do well in long, hot summers, while apples, pears, plums, gooseberries and currants need cooler conditions, especially in winter. Cold weather during late spring can damage buds, flowers and young shoots.

In very mild districts, the only option is to choose fruits that revel in heat. In cold gardens, note where frost lingers longest and plant elsewhere; never plant at the bottom of a slope, where cold air tends to collect. If you have no choice, plant taller

fruit trees and late flowering bush fruit varieties in the cold spots, reserving the warmer sites for smaller and earlier flowering plants.

■ **Strong winds discourage** pollinating insects, injure flowers and cause fruits to drop prematurely. The best protection is a

---

Fruit for small spaces

By using compact varieties and restricted forms, you can assemble a large amount of fruit in quite a small area. A garden about 6 x 4m (20 x 12ft) could include a row each of gooseberries, red currants and blackcurrants and two rows of raspberries. Loganberries, blackberries, fan-trained peaches and cordon apples and pears could be grown around the perimeter on posts and wires or along a fence.

In a tiny garden, you could plant cordon apples on very dwarfing rootstocks, 75cm (2ft 6in) apart against a fence; train three or four raspberry plants in a cluster round a post (see page 98); and plant a thornless cut-leaved blackberry to make an attractive arch. Strawberries are good edging plants, standard gooseberries and red currants are decorative highlights in flower borders, and many tree fruits will grow well in generous-sized pots.

hedge of beech, a row of trees such as willow or a windbreak of netting or open-board fencing. However, don't build a wall or a solid fence as this will block the wind and cause turbulence.

■ **A sunny situation is vital** for warm-climate crops, like peaches and greengages. Late ripening top, or tree, fruit also need the a lot of sunshine, whereas most soft fruits will tolerate some shade for up to half the day. You can train certain fruits on a fence or wall, saving space and allowing the fruits to benefit from the reflected warmth of the sun. Avoid areas of deep shade, especially under overhanging trees.

■ **Most soils are suitable** for growing fruit, provided they are well drained. You should dig heavy clay deeply to prevent waterlogging and work plenty of compost or well-rotted manure into light soils to improve water retention.

When to start Ideally, carry out preparation at the end of summer and during early autumn, clearing the weeds first and using weedkiller, if necessary, to get rid of any perennial weeds. In early autumn dig the ground, to allow it several weeks to settle before planting.

Pruning and training Top fruits, such as apples, pears and 'stone fruits' like plums, cherries and peaches, grow naturally into large trees, but you can prune and train most of them to create a more attractive and productive shape that occupies much less space (see also Rootstocks, above right). Soft fruits that can be pruned and trained into restricted shapes include bushes such as gooseberries and red and white currants.

■ **Tree fruits like apples, pears,** plums and cherries in most open ground can be trained as standards with 1.5–2.2m (5–7ft) trunks, half-standards with 1–1.5m (3–5ft) trunks, bushes with stems up to 1m (3ft) high and cone-shaped dwarf pyramids, 2.2–2.5m (7–8ft) high.

Rootstocks and fruit tree sizes

Most fruit trees are grafted onto a standardised rootstock, which controls the vigour of the tree and reduces its natural size. Some fruits, such as apples and, to a lesser degree, pears, are supplied on a range of rootstocks, from vigorous to very dwarfing, whereas only one or two kinds are available for plums, peaches and cherries. To get the most from a limited space, you need to combine a restrictive form of training with an appropriate rootstock. Good fruit catalogues list the rootstocks available, the trained forms they suit, and their ultimate sizes and recommended spacing.

■ **Gooseberries and red currants** are grown as bushes, with a 15cm (6in) stem, or as a standard with a 1–1.2m (3–4ft) stem.

■ **All tree and bush fruits** (with the exception of blackcurrants) can be trained to form cordons, espaliers and fans. They can be trained flat against walls and fences, or as freestanding specimens along wires stretched between posts. The commonest forms are cordons, which are upright or angled straight stems with short fruiting sideshoots; these are used for apples, pears, gooseberries and red or white currants. The same fruits are also suitable for growing as espaliers, which have a central trunk with pairs of opposite, horizontal branches. Fans, which have branches radiating from a short central trunk, are best for plums, cherries, figs, apricots and peaches; they also suit apples, pears and gooseberries.

■ **Blackberries and hybrid berries** can be grown flat on wires, informally or as neat fans, and thornless varieties on pillars and arches, like a climber.

Preparing the ground Unless your soil is already well cultivated, you will need to prepare the site thoroughly at least a month before planting. The best way to do this is in simple stages.

Raspberries for a small garden

To save space, plant four or five strong raspberry canes round a central post, buried 45–60cm (18–24in) in the ground. Tie the canes in a group with loops of string or, in windy gardens, attach them individually to vertical wires stapled to each face of the post. Grow and prune in the usual way.

■ **Mark out the fruit garden** area with canes and string or a garden line, marking approximate planting positions (these depend on fruit type and form).

■ **Spray weeds** with a systemic weedkiller such as glyphosate, and leave for three weeks for it to take full effect. Alternatively, fork out perennial weeds.

■ **Dig the whole area** – single digging is sufficient for good soil, but double digging is advisable for soil that is impoverished or overgrown with weeds, or on heavy soils where drainage is poor.

■ **Feed the soil and improve** drainage by digging in garden compost or well-rotted manure, spreading an 8cm (3in) layer in each trench as you dig.

■ **Leave the ground to settle** for at least a month before lightly forking and levelling the surface prior to planting.

Planting a bare-rooted tree Store bare-rooted trees safely if you can't plant them immediately. If they look dry, plunge the roots in a bucket of water for two to three hours before planting. Trim back any damaged roots, and shorten excessively long ones to 30cm (12in).

■ **Mark the planting position** of the tree with a cane, spacing it an adequate distance from any neighbours. Dig a hole large enough to take the roots comfortably when spread out, and at a depth that leaves the old soil mark on the stem at ground level.

■ **Drive in a vertical stake** 8–10cm (3–4in) off-centre and on the lee side of the tree (the side away from the prevailing wind). The top of the stake should reach a third of the way up the trunk, or up to the first branches in exposed positions.

■ **In a large bucket,** mix 5 litres (1 gallon) of planting mix, made up of equal parts of well-rotted manure and garden compost or leaf-mould, plus 140g (5oz) each of seaweed meal and bone meal. Fork this into the excavated topsoil.

When making a new bed in an old lawn, skim off the top 5–8cm (2–3in) of turf and bury upside-down in the planting hole.

■ **Hold the tree upright** in its hole, spread a few trowelfuls of the planting mix over the roots, and gently shake the tree up and down so that the mix settles. Repeat and firm the mix lightly with your foot.

■ **Half-fill the hole** with planting mix, and gently tread firm. Check that the tree is still at the right depth, then fill the hole up, firm again and level the surface. Attach the tree to its support with an adjustable tie fixed near the top of the stake. Water in well.

Planting a container-grown tree

Mark out the intended planting position of the tree, and dig out a hole large enough to allow for 10cm (4in) of planting mix below and all round the rootball.

■ **Water the plant thoroughly** and stand it in the hole on the layer of planting mix. Cut down the side of the container and remove it carefully.

■ **Fill in around the rootball** with planting mix, firming it as you go with your fists or a trowel handle; level the surface. Water in.

■ **Position the stake** on the side away from the prevailing wind. Drive the stake in at a 45-degree angle so that it avoids penetrating the roots, and secure the tree with an adjustable tie.

Soft fruit
Plant bush fruits in the same way as tree fruits, following the appropriate bare-rooted or container-grown method.

■ **Bury blackcurrants** 5–8cm (2–3in) lower than their original growing depth to encourage branching from below ground.

■ **Staking is unnecessary,** except for standard red currants and gooseberries, which need supporting with stakes and adjustable ties near the top of their stem.

■ **Blackberries, raspberries** and fan or cordon-trained gooseberries and currants need tying in to a system of horizontal wires attached to vertical posts, or to vine eyes screwed into a wall or fence.

■ **Raspberries dislike wet soils:** where drainage is poor, spread builders' rubble or gravel into the hole as you dig, or add extra topsoil to create planting ridges 8–10cm (3–4in) high.

After planting
Some fruits need pruning at planting time to stimulate plenty of new growth where it is needed.

■ **You do not have to prune** fruit trees at planting time, unless you are training a restricted form such as a fan or espalier from a one-year-old tree (maiden).

■ **Cut down all stems** of blackcurrant to 2–3cm (1in) high after planting.

■ **Prune the main stems** on gooseberry and red or white currant bushes by half, making the cuts just above outward-facing buds.

■ **Cut raspberries down** to a bud about 23cm (9in) above the ground.

For best results, keep an area about 1m (3ft) around the fruits weed-free for at least the first two to three seasons. Do this by hoeing, spraying with weedkiller, or by mulching with manure or compost. Water regularly in dry periods, especially if the soil is light; continue this until the beginning of winter for bush fruits, and for one to two years for tree fruits. Feed plants every spring, and prune at the appropriate season for shapely, productive plants.

Plant raspberries so that the canes sit at the same depth they were growing previously, or 5cm (2in) deeper on light sandy soils.

Autumn is a productive time in the kitchen garden, when your hard work earlier in the year pays off and many fruit and vegetables are ready to be harvested. And if you're lucky, and it's been a bumper year, it can also be a busy time in the kitchen, as you freeze and preserve your excess produce.

Bay

Laurus nobilis

Large evergreen shrub or small tree with creamy white flowers in very hot summers. The leaves are used to flavour soups, stews and stocks. Use fresh or harvest to dry in early summer. Fairly hardy when established, but frost-sensitive while young and in exposed gardens.

Site Sun, sheltered. Well-drained soil. Grow in pots of soil-based (John Innes No. 3) compost with good drainage.

How to grow Plant in spring or autumn and protect from frosts for two years. Water regularly in dry summers.

Blackberry

Rubus fruticosus

Cultivated blackberries are vigorous and need firm training on wires or a fence. A range of varieties offers fruit from late summer until the frosts. Hardy.

Site Sun, sheltered. Fertile, well-drained soil
How to grow Plant while dormant, spacing the plants 4m (12ft) apart. Water in dry

weather, and feed and mulch in spring. Train in new canes and prune out fruited ones after harvesting ripe fruit.

Brussels sprout

Brassica oleracea Gemmifera Group

Sprouts are normally picked after the first frost, which improves their flavour. Firm ground or staking is essential for taller varieties. Hardy.

Site Sun, light shade. Deep, rich very firm soil, limed to pH7 or higher.

How to grow Sow seed outdoors in mid spring. Thin seedlings to 8cm (3in) apart and transplant 60cm (2ft) apart each way when five or six weeks old. Water freely in dry weather. Feed with high-nitrogen fertiliser in midsummer. Remove yellowing leaves and net against birds.

Cabbage, autumn

Brassica oleracea Capitata Group

Hardier and slower growing than summer cabbage, this produces large heads that remain in good condition for weeks. Hardy.

Site Sun. Rich firm soil; add lime if acid.

How to grow Sow outdoors in mid spring. Thin seedlings to 8cm (3in) apart and transplant 50cm (20in) apart, less for compact varieties, when six to eight weeks old; plant firmly. Water in dry weather and protect from birds. Cut heads off when large enough. If frost threatens, dig up mature heads and hang in a cool frost-free place.

Carrot, maincrop

Daucus carota

Maincrop carrots are autumn and winter varieties, sown later than summer kinds, that grow for at least 12 weeks. Whole crops can be dug up for storing when mature, but

in mild gardens with light soils, roots remain sound over winter if mulched. Hardy.
Site Sun. Light, well-drained soil with plenty of added compost.
How to grow Sow seed outdoors in late spring, in rows 15cm (6in) apart. Thin seedlings to 5–8cm (2–3in) apart and mulch. Water every two to three weeks in dry weather. Fork up roots when large enough. Twist off tops and store in boxes in damp sand, or mulch rows with straw or leaves 15cm (6in) deep, held down with net or soil.

Grape

Vitis vinifera and *Vitis* cultivars

Outdoor dessert grapes are best trained on a warm wall; wine grapes are hardier and can crop heavily after a hot summer. Good

varieties include 'Siegerrebe' (white) and 'Brant' (black, good autumn colour). Hardy.
Site Sun, sheltered. Well-drained good soil.
How to grow Plant 1.2–1.5m (4–5ft) apart while dormant. Train on wires. Mulch in spring with rotted manure. Water regularly in dry weather. Prune after fruiting, cutting all sideshoots back to the main branches.

Jerusalem artichoke

Helianthus tuberosus

This produces nutritious tubers and tall leafy stems, which make an effective windbreak if grown in rows. Stems can be shortened in

midsummer to 2m (6ft). 'Fuseau' has the smoothest tubers. Hardy.
Site Sun, light shade. Fertile soil with plenty of added compost.

How to grow Plant small tubers in early spring, 10–15cm (4–6in) deep and 30cm (12in) apart. Water freely in dry weather. Earth and mulch stems for extra support. For larger tubers remove flowers. Lift as required from very early autumn.

Kohl rabi

Brassica oleracea Gongylodes Group

This cabbage relative has smooth swollen stems that are crisp and mildly flavoured. Ready just seven to eight weeks after sowing, even on soils too dry for other brassicas. The 'bulbs' are best when the size of tennis balls, although modern varieties grown on moist soils remain crisp when much larger. Not fully hardy.
Site Light shade. Fertile sandy soil.
How to grow Sow small batches of seed every three to four weeks in rows 30cm (12in) apart, from mid-spring until midsummer. Thin seedlings to 15–20cm (6–8in) apart. Water regularly in dry weather and mulch. Pull plants when large enough. Late crops can be stored in boxes of sand, or left outdoors in mild weather.

Leek, early

Allium porrum

Mild-flavoured member of the onion family with non-bulbing white stems. Early varieties, such as 'Albinstar' and 'King Richard', are juicy but cannot withstand frost. Mini-leeks, grown by thinning leek seedlings to 2.5cm (1in) apart, are ready when the size of spring onions. Tender.
Site Sun, light shade. Deep rich soil with plenty of added compost.
How to grow Sow seed under glass in late winter then prick out into trays, or outdoors in mid spring, thinning seedlings to 4cm (1½in) apart. Plant out from late spring onwards, when 20cm (8in) high, dropping single seedlings into 15cm (6in) deep holes, spaced 15cm (6in) apart in rows 30cm (12in) apart. Water occasionally in dry weather. Lift in autumn, when large enough.

Marrow

Cucurbita pepo

Marrows can be cut eight weeks after planting and will crop until the first frosts. The last can be 'cured' (see below), then stored in a dry airy place at about 10ºC (50ºF) for several weeks. Trailing varieties can be planted on a compost heap. Tender.
Site Sun, sheltered. Rich, deeply dug soil with plenty of added compost.

How to grow Sow seed indoors in small pots two to three weeks before the last frosts and plant out when all risk of frost is past. Space bush varieties 1–1.2m (3–4ft) apart and trailing kinds 2m (6ft) apart. Water and mulch liberally. Pinch out trailing kinds when five leaves have opened and spread out resulting sideshoots across the ground or tie to trellis. Harvest regularly. To 'cure' for storing, dry fruits in the sun in a greenhouse or on a windowsill for two weeks.

Onion, maincrop

Allium cepa

Can be raised from seed or, more easily, from sets (immature bulbs). A combination of spring and autumn sowing or planting can ensure a year-round supply. Half hardy.
Site Sun. Fertile, well-drained soil with plenty of added compost.
How to grow Sow seed in early spring in rows 30cm (12in) apart. Thin seedlings to 5cm (2in) apart for small bulbs and 10–15cm (4–6in) for large ones. Plant sets at the same distances, with tips just covered. Water frequently until midsummer. In late summer to early autumn fork up bulbs carefully and spread out on trays or under glass to dry. When skins are papery, store in nets or boxes; they will keep until spring.

Potato, maincrop

Solanum tuberosum

Maincrop potatoes yield heavily on most soils. Although they occupy space for most of the growing season, they can be stored until spring. Good varieties are 'Marfona', 'Cara', 'Romano' and 'Picasso'. Not fully hardy.
Site Sun. Fertile, deeply dug and well-drained soil.
How to grow 'Chit' seed potatoes in late winter and plant out in mid spring 10–15cm (4–6in) deep, 40cm (16in) apart in rows 75cm (2ft 6in) apart. Mound soil half-way up stems every two to three weeks until leaves of adjacent plants meet. Water well once or twice after flowering starts. Cut down the

foliage when it turns brown in autumn, then lift the tubers with a fork two weeks later. Allow to dry on the surface for a few hours, then store in an insulated clamp or in thick paper sacks in a cool dry place.

Quince
Cydonia oblonga
Small tree bearing perfumed golden pear or apple-shaped fruits in autumn. Bush, standard trees and fans for training on a wall are available. Look for 'Vranja' and 'Meech's Prolific'. Hardy.

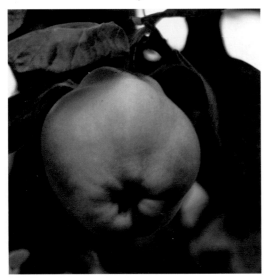

Site Sun, sheltered. Deep, light, fertile soil.
How to grow Plant while dormant, 4.5–6m (15–20ft) apart. Feed or mulch with rotted manure annually in early spring. Prune in winter, removing misplaced, crossing and congested shoots. Leave fruits until fully coloured but harvest before frosts. Store in boxes in a cool airy place for a month to allow the flavour to develop; keep away from other fruit to avoid cross-flavouring.

Squash, winter
Cucurbita maxima and C. moschata
Vigorous trailing plants that need plenty of space, but tolerate light shade so make good ground cover. Pumpkins and other winter squashes can be stored for months over winter. Tender.

Site Sun, light shade. Rich, well dug soil with added compost or rotted manure.
How to grow Sow and plant as for marrows or sow in situ after the last frosts. Water well in dry weather and feed every two to three weeks while fruits are swelling. To grow large squashes, thin fruitlets to three to four on each plant. Move or remove leaves to expose ripening fruits to the sun. Cut when large enough or, for storing, leave until fully coloured in early autumn. Cure and store as for marrows.

Raspberry, autumn
Rubus idaeus
Autumn-fruiting raspberries yield heavy crops of firm red, sometimes golden fruits until the frosts. They produce a dense screen of tall canes. Try 'Autumn Bliss', 'Heritage' or yellow 'Fallgold'. Hardy.
Site Sun. Deep, light soil with added compost.
How to grow Plant while dormant, 45–60cm (18–24in) apart in rows 1.2m (4ft) apart, and cut down to 23cm (9in) high. In early spring feed and mulch with compost. Train in canes as they grow, fanning them evenly about 10cm (4in) apart on parallel wires. Harvest fruit when fully coloured. Leave canes over winter, cutting to ground level in late winter to allow for new season's canes.

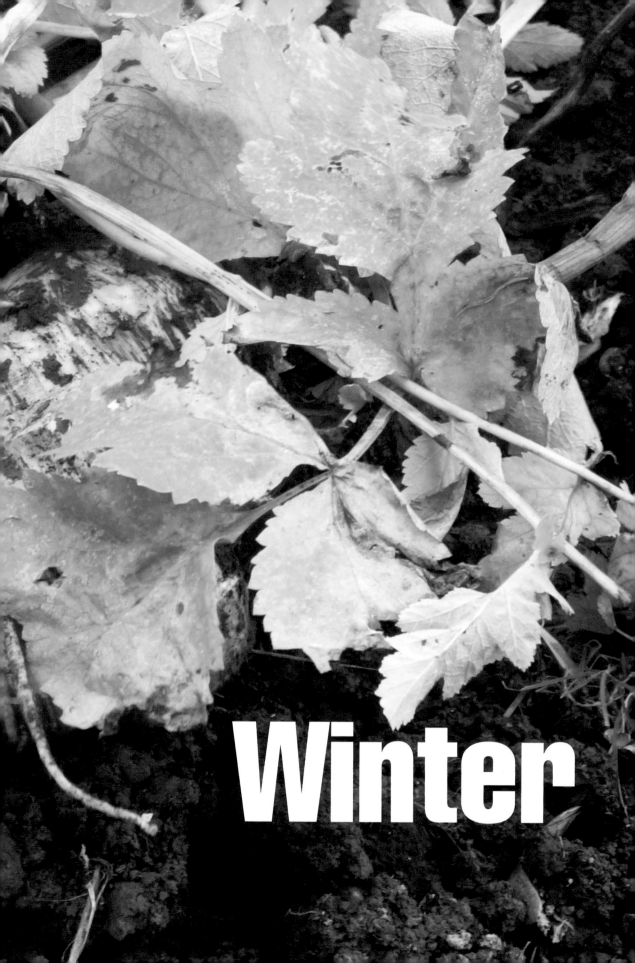

Winter

While many vegetables have now been picked and stored away, there will still be some fresh crops to pick. Take advantage of mild spells to dig and prepare seedbeds and, when the weather keeps you indoors, draw up plans for next year so you have time to order seeds, young plants and potatoes.

Winter checklist

■ **Plan next year's** crop rotation (see page 112) and order seeds and potatoes for the coming season.

■ **Create a seedbed** early in winter. Cover the area with plastic sheeting to warm the soil for early crops (see opposite).

■ **Hoe off** weed seedlings.

■ **Watch for pests** and diseases in mild periods. Look for aphids hiding in the outer leaves of cabbages, cauliflowers and other overwintering vegetables.

■ **Control slugs** with baits or chemicals if necessary. Young slugs start feeding on plants almost immediately the eggs hatch during warm spells.

■ **Watch for bird damage:** crops will be attacked as food supplies become scarce, and hungry wood pigeons can devastate a crop of cauliflowers. Protect vegetables with netting or use bird scarers. A length of twine or old video tape stretched just above the crop deters many birds – but not wood pigeons, which tend to walk in to feed, rather than fly direct.

■ **Use stored vegetables** and check those that remain; discard any with signs of mould or rot. Watch for vermin damage, as mice nest and feed in stores during cold periods.

■ **Check storage temperatures:** if stored vegetables start to sprout, this indicates the store is too warm and produce will deteriorate rapidly.

■ **Put cloches in place** or low polythene tunnels to warm the soil and help it to dry out after wet weather.

■ **Make early sowings** of beetroot, broad beans, carrots, lettuce, peas, radishes, spinach or turnips when the soil has had a chance to warm sufficiently and spring is approaching.

Harvesting now
■ Brussels sprouts
■ Celeriac
■ Jerusalem artichokes
■ Kale
■ Leeks
■ Parsnips
■ Swedes
■ Winter cabbage
■ Winter cauliflower
■ Winter radish
■ Winter spinach

Winter cultivation

Complete the winter digging on mild days, when weather conditions allow. The heavier the soil, the earlier it should be dug to let frost break it down; lighter, free-draining soils can be left until later. The depth of cultivation depends on your soil and the plants you plan to grow.

Single digging Single digging is ideal for shallow-rooted salad crops, such as lettuce, and small, round-rooted vegetables like beetroot. It entails digging trenches to a depth of about 30cm (12in), or one spade blade deep and wide. Work systematically across the plot; bury any plant debris and old mulch from the surface in the base of the previously opened trench, and cover it with soil as you dig the next one.

Double digging Double digging improves poor drainage and is good preparation for deep-rooted crops, such as carrots and parsnips, and long-term crops like asparagus and rhubarb. It is similar to single digging but more strenuous, as you cultivate to approximately 60cm (2ft) or the depth of two spade blades. Well-rotted manure or garden compost is forked into the base of each trench. It is important to avoid mixing the darker topsoil with the paler, infertile subsoil as you work.

Preparing a seedbed

Dig over the soil in the vegetable patch in late autumn or early winter, especially if it is heavy. Roughly level the surface and leave for a month or two so that frosts can break up the clods and make final preparation easier. This time lag also allows weeds to germinate, for easy removal later on.

Two or three weeks before you intend to sow vegetable seeds, when the weather is fair and the soil is not so wet that it clings to your tools, lightly fork over the surface

Double digging incorporates well-rotted manure or garden compost, giving root crops a good start.

to break up any remaining clods and then rake the surface level (see below).

Once you have prepared the seedbed, it is necessary to warm the soil by covering it with cloches, low polythene tunnels or black or clear plastic sheeting. Black plastic excludes light and heats up the soil more quickly, whereas the advantage of clear plastic is that it provides ideal conditions for weed seeds to germinate, for easier removal before sowing.

TIP If you plan to sow early, don't be tempted to sow seeds in periods of mild weather during late winter without first checking that the soil temperature is correct. Many seeds need the soil to be between 5–7°C (40–45°F) before they will germinate. Insert a thermometer into the top 8–10cm (3–4in) of soil regularly and check the reading (see page 10).

Making a seedbed

1 Using the back of a fork, break up any lumps of soil on the prepared bed. Next, rake the surface until it is fine and level.

2 For early sowings, you must first warm the soil. Cover the seedbed with plastic sheeting, spreading it over upturned plant pots so that condensation drains to the edges rather than dripping on the prepared surface.

3 After two or threee weeks hoe off any seedling weeds, disturbing the soil as little as possible, or treat with weedkiller for a clean start.

Winter crops

Early winter is the time to order seeds and young plants from catalogues. By late winter you can begin to sow for the year ahead in pots or cellular trays under cover and outside, if conditions are suitable. The success of your vegetable garden hinges on careful planning, in terms of what you choose to grow and how you operate your crop rotations (see pages 111–13).

Peas and beans Inspect autumn-sown broad beans in spells of very cold weather and protect the plants with cloches or a covering of horticultural fleece.
- **Sow broad beans** into 8–10cm (3–4in) pots, one or two per pot, in a cool greenhouse. Transplant in early spring.
- **Check autumn-sown** peas under cloches and insulate with thick fleece or a layer of loose straw if very cold days and nights are anticipated.
- **Sow early varieties** of peas in 8–10cm (3–4in) pots, two or three per pot, in a cool greenhouse. These will be large enough for transplanting in mid-March to crop in May. Sow early peas outdoors under cloches to follow on the batches you have raised under glass.

Autumn-sown broad beans may need to be protected with fleece.

Cabbage family Harvest brussels sprouts: pick the largest first from the base and work up the stem. Support the plants with short canes and string ties to prevent them from blowing over. Pick the leafy tops for eating and to reduce vulnerability to wind rock.
- **When harvesting kale,** remove and compost larger outer leaves each time the young shoots are picked over.

- **Cut winter cabbages as** required. Cut off the head, leaving 8–10cm (3–4in) of stalk protruding from the ground. Cross-cut these stalks to encourage a secondary crop of leafy greens in mid-spring.
- **In cold spells,** protect spring cabbages from pigeons and other birds by covering the crop with nets or by using bird scarers.

Pests may strip the leaves of brussels sprouts, but this will have no detrimental effect on the sprouts.

Onion family Use stored onions, shallots and garlic. Check bulbs and remove any that show signs of rot or mould.
- **The last chance** to plant garlic is in February. Plant cloves 2–3cm (1in) deep and spaced 15–20cm (6–8in) apart, on a ridge if your soil is heavy.
- **Plant shallots** from December to March. Plant the small bulbs, or sets, setting them 1cm (½in) deep and 10–15cm (4–6in) apart.

Jumbo garlic cloves can be planted in cellular trays under glass, to plant outdoors once they have sprouted.

■ **Lift mature leeks** as required during mild spells; lifting them when the ground is frozen will cause bruising and stem rot.

■ **Sow leeks and onions** in cellular trays or small pots during late winter. Place in a cool greenhouse; sow four or five onion seeds per pot for transplanting in mid-spring.

Potatoes and root crops Use carrots and beetroot in store, discarding any that are showing signs of rot.

■ **Lift celeriac, parsnip** and winter radish as required when the weather is mild and the soil is not frozen or waterlogged. If a cold spell is forecast, lift and store some roots in a shed so they are ready for use.

■ **Sow early varieties** of beetroot, carrot and turnip in open ground if the soil conditions are suitable. Pre-warming the soil and cloche protection will be necessary in all but the mildest gardens.

■ **Sow celeriac in late winter** in cellular trays in a cool greenhouse for transplanting in late spring.

■ **Order seed potatoes** in good time and chit early varieties indoors from February.

Salad crops Protect overwintering lettuce with cloches or low polythene tunnels, allowing some ventilation to reduce the risk of fungal rots developing.

■ **Sow short rows** of lettuce, radish and spinach in late winter under cloches on previously warmed soil.

Other crops Lift jerusalem artichoke tubers as required. If cold weather is forecast, lift and temporarily store some for immediate use.

Rows of lettuce seedlings are protected in a coldframe. Pick alternate plants and allow the others to develop a heart.

■ **Order asparagus crowns** for planting in early spring. Prepare planting trenches for the new beds by double digging.

Starting a vegetable plot

It is possible to include a few favourite vegetables almost anywhere in the garden, but the time may come when you want to grow a more ambitious selection of crops in a dedicated kitchen garden or vegetable plot.

The right site Choosing the best place to grow vegetables is important, as it can make the difference between success and failure.

■ **Provide shelter from cold winds** that can affect cropping; even light winds reduce yields by 20 per cent or more, especially during winter. Fences and hedges bordering the vegetable plot can filter winds and limit their impact, protecting fruit and vegetable crops, and increasing productivity.

■ **Walls can be a mixed blessing.** They are valuable for supporting trained fruit, but solid barriers can produce strong wind turbulence within the garden and trap frost. Make sure boundary or internal walls do not affect the proposed site adversely.

■ **Plenty of sunlight** is needed, particularly by winter crops, to yield well.

■ **Light shade in summer** prevents leafy vegetables like lettuce and kohl rabi from drying out, but heavy shade from buildings or trees is best avoided.

■ **Good drainage** is essential. Heavy, waterlogged soil causes all kinds of problems for vegetables. If puddles remain on the surface, you might have to dig the site deeply to improve drainage, or consider raising the soil level in beds or ridges to increase the depth of well-drained earth.

■ **Soil can be improved** over time by incorporating large amounts of organic material, such as garden compost and well-rotted manure. This adds body to light soils and opens up heavy clays. With regular cultivating and mulching, your soil and crops will steadily improve in quality.

Making a traditional vegetable plot

You will need: spade, rake, string and pegs, measuring tape, 16 treated timber boards 8–10cm (3–4in) wide by 2.5cm (1in) thick, 16 battens 30cm (12in) long, sledgehammer, screwdriver and screws, cocoa shells and grit, or bark.

1 Dig the whole site, removing as many weeds as possible, especially the roots of perennial species. Rake the area level.

2 Using the string and pegs, mark out the plot as a square. Divide this into quarters by marking out two central paths 50cm (20in) wide, crossing at right angles in the centre.

3 Drive the battens firmly into the ground at the corners of the beds. Push the treated boards into the soil to edge the beds; screw to the battens.

4 Surface the paths with a layer of cocoa shells and grit or shredded bark. For a permanent surface, such as brick or slabs, dig out some of the soil and spread this on the beds before laying the paving material.

5 Allocate beds as 1, 2, 3 or 4 for crop rotation (see page 112) and fork in the following: rotted manure in bed 1 for peas and beans; garden compost and fertiliser in bed 2 for potatoes; and compost and fertiliser in bed 4 for brassicas. Rake fertiliser into bed 3 for root crops. Rake all the beds level.

6 Plant any edging crops of perennial herbs, flowers or low hedges and water the beds. You are now ready to plan plantings of vegetables for each bed.

■ **Plot size** will influence the plants you will be able grow, though even a small area can be productive. If you have a small plot, choose vegetables that grow close together. Include tall varieties that use vertical space, like beans, and crop the ground intensively by close-spacing the plants.

A practical design In drawing up a plan for your vegetable plot, do your best to incorporate the permanent features detailed below. Some of these will make your day-to-day gardening easier, while others, like paths, form a key part of the layout.

■ **One or two compost bins** will allow you to dispose of annual weeds and vegetable waste, returning their fertility to the garden.

■ **Leave enough space** to stack manure, leaf-mould and other bulky materials for digging into and improving the soil.

■ **Consider installing a tap** and standpipe, or a tank to collect rainwater, so you don't have to carry water too far.

■ **A coldframe is useful** for protecting early crops or heating the soil before planting out.

■ **Include borders or other space** for herbs and perennial vegetables, such as asparagus and globe artichokes.

■ **Many fruits are permanent** and should be considered early in the planning stage.

■ **Paths provide essential** access for cultivation and for harvesting, particularly on a wet day. Depending on plot size, you will need at least one all-weather path, ideally wide enough to take a wheelbarrow. Narrower paths between beds can be of beaten earth or more durable materials.

■ **Edges to beds,** such as treated timber boards, bricks or a low hedge of perennial herbs, will help keep the paths clean.

Style and layout There are alternative layouts to the traditional one shown left, which make efficient use of the space. And a vegetable garden need not always be strictly functional, as many crops are ornamental as well as edible.

Every kitchen garden should have at least one compost bin to transform waste material into a valuable soil conditioner.

■ **Traditional kitchen gardens** are quartered by crossing paths, a system that allows for efficient crop rotation and a large number of bed edges to plant with herbs, fruit or flowers for cutting.

■ **Raised or narrow beds,** up to 1.2m (4ft) wide, are very productive; they make the most of small spaces and organic matter and are useful in planning crop rotations, too. Several can be arranged to form a kitchen garden, or you can include them as an integral part of a flower border.

■ **Potagers are plots** that exploit the decorative potential of vegetables by arranging them like bedding plants, balancing their shapes and colours in a pattern of formally shaped beds.

■ **A cottage garden** patchwork can be made by organising small square beds in a flexible layout for any size or shape of site, perhaps combined with flowers.

Crop rotation Growing vegetables in a new position each year is an important precaution against building up soil pests and diseases, and depleting soil nutrients. The traditional method is to divide the ground into three or four plots or beds, then move groups of vegetables with similar needs and disorders from one bed to the next in annual sequence. The three main groups are legumes (peas and beans), brassicas (the cabbage family), and root crops, including onions, with potatoes and squashes in a fourth bed. Fit in salad leaves and sweetcorn wherever there is space. Additions of rotted manure or garden compost are made to each bed when digging and preparing it for planting, depending on the type of crop grown in it (see below). Fertiliser, where required, is applied just before planting the crop. In small gardens, where only a few vegetables are grown, simply avoid growing a particular group or individual crop in the same place for two consecutive years.

No-dig beds The deep bed, or no-dig, system of cultivation is based on the concept that routine cultivation damages the soil structure and can lead to a reduction in the population of worms and other beneficial organisms within the soil. Instead of digging the soil to work in organic matter, the organic matter is spread over the surface and left for worms and other organisms to gradually draw it down into the upper layers, improving fertility in the area penetrated by most plant roots. Worm activity not only breaks down organic matter but improves the soil's aeration, drainage and water-holding capacity.

The no-dig system is ideal for dealing with heavy clay soils, which are difficult to work and are easily compacted. By protecting the surface with organic matter structural damage is avoided. Below the surface, worms open up the soil's close structure and improve its drainage.

A once-only, thorough cultivation is essential to the success of the no-dig system. Double digging, incorporating large quantities of organic matter, enriches the soil and improves texture. But from this point on, any cultivation and walking on beds must be avoided to prevent disturbance or compaction, and to allow a natural soil structure to develop. For this reason, you need to be able to reach to the middle of the bed comfortably from either side, which limits the width to about 1.2m (4ft).

Maintenance of no-dig beds After the initial preparation is done you should mulch annually (see right). After harvesting leafy vegetables, leave the roots in the soil to decay naturally, trim vegetables near to where they were growing, and lay any leaf litter or waste on vacant areas of the bed to rot down.

Rotation groups

	YEAR 1	YEAR 2	YEAR 3	YEAR 4
BED ONE	Legumes (add well-rotted manure)	Brassicas (add compost and fertiliser)	Roots and onions (add fertiliser)	Potatoes (add manure or compost and fertiliser)
BED TWO	Potatoes (add manure or compost and fertiliser)	Legumes (add well-rotted manure)	Brassicas (add compost and fertiliser)	Roots and onions (add fertiliser)
BED THREE	Roots and onions (add fertiliser)	Potatoes (add manure or compost and fertiliser)	Legumes (add well-rotted manure)	Brassicas (add compost and fertiliser)
BED FOUR	Brassicas (add compost and fertiliser)	Roots and onions (add fertiliser)	Potatoes (add manure or compost and fertiliser)	Legumes (add well-rotted manure)

Maintaining a no-dig bed

1 Mulch the surface to a depth of 10cm (4in) every year with well-rotted organic matter to keep soil fertile. This deep mulching will reduce moisture loss, suppress the germination of weed seeds and keep the soil warmer, extending the growing season. Always work from a path.

2 Scrape back the mulch to expose the soil surface when you are ready to plant, then replace it afterwards, keeping it clear of young stems. The timber edging helps to retain the mulch layer within the bed until it rots down.

Choosing the crops To some extent, deciding what to grow is a matter of trial and error. Start with vegetables that are family favourites and also those that are expensive or hard to find in the shops.

■ **List your favourite** vegetables and decide what not to grow. Good quality maincrop potatoes and cabbages may be available locally, whereas salad leaves, sweetcorn or early baby carrots taste better picked fresh.

■ **Match your list** to the available space and the time and energy you can devote to their cultivation. Recognise the difference between vegetables that sprint to maturity, allowing you to grow something else afterwards, and slow crops such as brussels sprouts that need a long growing season.

■ **Use your space** to best effect. Do you want to harvest a wide variety of produce for as long as possible, or simply to raise large amounts of a few varieties for storing or self-indulgence?

Narrow beds, edged by boards, are one way to grow vegetables in a small space. The soil level drops slightly as the organic matter rots.

■ **Find out what does well** locally. As your soil and skills improve, your range of produce will increase, but some crops may not suit your ground or local climate.

■ **Keep a garden diary** and note your most successful crops and varieties, with their sowing or planting dates, to help you plan for the future years.

Raising from seed The cheapest and most rewarding way to grow vegetables is to raise them from seed, but this depends on having a greenhouse, or at least a coldframe, to start plants off in the warmth. Growing from seed also gives you a wider choice of vegetables and allows you to select more unusual varieties.

Buying plug plants Where space is at a premium, it is a good idea to visit a garden centre and buy plug plants or small trays of seedlings. This allows you to buy just as many plants as you have space to grow, without the trouble of raising them from seed. You can buy a wide range of crops in this form, both direct and through mail-order and internet outlets.

Turnips take up relatively little space in the vegetable plot and the leafy tops can be cooked and eaten as greens.

Plug plants and seedlings are an invaluable way of raising vegetables if you do not have a greenhouse or coldframe, and prefer not to fill your windowsills with propagating cases and pots of seedlings early each year. Instead, let the professionals germinate the seeds and grow on the young plants in controlled conditions. You can take over in spring, when growing conditions are more favourable for young plants.

Cropping continuity The challenge of vegetable growing is having a range of crops available for the kitchen all year round. There are various ways in which you can make the most of your vegetable plot and keep it healthy.

■ **Successional sowing** of quick-maturing crops like spinach, beetroot, radishes and lettuce helps to prevent gluts and gaps. Sow small amounts of seed at regular intervals. Timing can be difficult to gauge, but a good guide is to sow a new batch of seed when the first true leaves (those forming after the seed leaves) start to emerge on the previous sowing. In this way you avoid 'bolting' lettuces, woody roots or bitter spinach leaves.

■ **Intercropping means using** the space between slow-growing crops as a seedbed for vegetables that will later need transplanting or are quick maturing. Radishes, rocket, lettuce, turnips and beetroot (pulled young) are all suitable for growing between crops such as winter cabbages, brussels sprouts or parsnips, spaced a little further apart than usual.

■ **Catch crops** – a 'catch' or quick-maturing crop – take advantage of vacant soil. For example, rapidly maturing lettuce, spinach or peas could precede a tender crop of runner beans, tomatoes, sweetcorn or courgettes, none of which can be planted in the ground until the risk of frost is over. The catch crop is harvested before the tender crop is planted, or at least before it gets established.

Quick-maturing spring onions and lettuces are grown here as an intercrop between rows of slower growing main crop carrots.

Maximising your space Make full use of available ground by spacing plants equally in each direction rather than in rows. This planting 'on the square' (or in staggered rows) works well in a bed system, where equally spaced plants grow evenly and weeds are quickly crowded out. You can also space plants closer than recommended to produce 'baby' vegetables, a method particularly suited to root crops.

Vegetables in small gardens If you have a really tiny garden that cannot encompass dedicated vegetable beds, it is still possible to grow a few vegetables. Here are some ideas, but try to experiment, too.

■ **Flower borders** are an ideal site for vegetables with handsome foliage, which will look attractive among the flowers. There are varieties of chard with rainbow-coloured stems in yellow, orange, pink and ruby red, while beetroots have dark, red-veined leaves and stems. Carrot foliage is soft and ferny, and in winter there are few plants that can match the majestic curly kale. Spinach beet and frilly, loose-leaved lettuces are always worth growing as cut-and-come-again crops. Sweetcorn is another possibility, planted in a group in a sunny spot. Runner or climbing

french beans trained up vertical canes at the back of a border, or along a boundary, give both privacy and produce during summer months. Don't expect the yields to be quite as high as they would be in a dedicated vegetable plot, however.

■ **Containers will accommodate** many types of vegetable. Tomatoes, salad crops, peas, beans, courgettes and squashes are easy to grow in large containers. Early potatoes are particularly successful when grown in a deep, barrel-like container. Fill it about a third full of soil-based compost, space out the sprouted seed tubers and cover with more compost. As the foliage appears, earth it up with more compost until the container is full. To harvest, scrape away the compost and lift a helping at a time, then cover up the remaining potatoes to grow on.

■ **Window boxes are ideal** for growing shallow-rooted crops, although carrot varieties with ball-like roots and radishes should also succeed. Peppers and cherry tomatoes crop well in a sunny aspect, so long as they are well fed and watered. Bush tomato varieties like 'Tumbler' need no training and will even grow successfully in a hanging basket. Lettuces and salad leaves do best on a windowsill shaded from the midday summer sun.

Vegetables in containers

Vegetables grown in containers must be watered regularly (daily in hot weather) and fed every 7–14 days with an appropriate fertiliser if they are to do well.

■ Feed fruiting crops like tomatoes, beans, courgettes, peppers, aubergines and cucumbers with a tomato fertiliser, which is high in phosphate and potash, to develop flowers and seeds.

■ Leafy vegetables, such as spinach, ruby chard, cut-and-come-again salad crops and lettuces, need a high-nitrogen feed to promote leafy growth.

Except for a few evergreens, most garden herbs will have died down by now. However, herbs growing in pots can provide fresh pickings during the winter months. Most herb care is confined under glass, but outside you can rejuvenate leggy sage and thyme, and prepare to make early sowings.

Winter checklist

■ **Ventilate herbs** growing under glass in mild weather as a precaution against fungal disease.

■ **Water sparingly** lemon verbena and other overwintering tender herbs.

■ **Lay hard paths** in a new herb garden and start constructing new beds.

■ **Protect containerised** herbs growing outdoors. In severe weather, bring the most vulnerable indoors or gather pots together and cover with fleece or bubble plastic.

■ **In early winter,** pot up root cuttings of mint and tarragon for fresh early supplies.

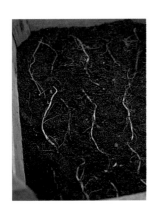

Put root cuttings of mint in a box of compost to force under glass.

■ **Order seeds** of annual herbs in good time.

■ **Clear annual** crops and tidy beds. Mulch with garden compost or well-rotted manure, which can be forked in before sowing in early spring.

■ **Cultivate new beds** for annual herbs.

■ **Prepare a mint bed** where the roots will not invade other plants. Buy mint plants in late winter or lift and divide existing healthy roots for replanting 30cm (12in) apart.

■ **Propagate old leggy plants** of sage, thyme and other woody herbs by mound layering or dropping (see opposite).

■ **Protect bay trees** from cold and remedy any frost damage in late winter.

■ **Cover a few parsley** and chive plants with cloches to revive growth ready for early pickings in spring.

Bay trees in winter

The shallow roots of bay trees less than three or four years old are vulnerable to frost, and severe cold weather can scorch the foliage. To guard against injury, plant bay in a sunny, sheltered position and screen from cold winds. In winter, bring potted bay plants indoors, or protect both plant and container with fleece or bubble plastic and clad bare stems in foam pipe insulation.

Bay trees are susceptible to frost, which can scorch their leaves in severe winters.

A thick mulch of leaf-mould or straw over the roots helps to prevent freezing in pots or open ground.

■ **If a few leaves** turn brown, remove them but leave shoots intact in case fresh growth appears later in the year.

■ **Extensive leaf browning** usually indicates the death of the top growth, but provided roots have been kept frost-free, new shoots may sprout from the base. Cut down the tree at the end of winter, leaving stumps 10cm (4in) long, and apply a balanced fertiliser.

Growing annual herbs

Annual or biennial herbs such as parsley, chervil and dill are usually sown in rows or in a special bed within the kitchen garden. Every two or three years it is advisable to prepare a new bed in a different position.

■ **Dig clay soil** in autumn, leave it rough and break it up finely with a fork in late winter. Add plenty of leaf-mould or garden compost to improve texture and drainage.

■ **Dig light soils** in late winter, adding plenty of garden compost or well-rotted manure to improve water retention.

■ **Before sowing** or planting, fork a balanced fertiliser into the top 8cm (3in) of soil. Rake to leave a fine, level seedbed.

Propagating leggy herbs

If woody herbs become leggy and bare at the base, take cuttings or layer some of the lower branches, then discard the old plants. 'Dropping' (see below) or mound layering in late winter will give you numerous new plants and improve the appearance of the parent. Dropping is best suited to sage, rosemary and lavender.

Mound layering This works well for thymes as well as other small, woody herbs.

■ **Mix together equal parts** of soil-based compost and grit and heap it over the bare centre of the plant, working it well in between the branches.

Annual and biennial herbs

To raise from seed
- Basil
- Borage
- Caraway
- Chervil
- Coriander
- Dill
- Parsley
- Summer savory

■ **Keep the plant** moist in dry weather.

■ **In early autumn,** carefully explore around the branches, most of which will have formed roots. These layers can now be detached for transplanting.

Dropping a rosemary

1 In late winter or early spring, dig up the leggy plant and excavate the hole 30cm (12in) deeper than it was previously.

2 Replant in the same hole, spreading out the branches. Return the soil to cover the centre of the plant and the bare portions of the branches.

3 Keep moist in dry weather and transplant any rooted layers in autumn, or leave them to form a wider clump.

With all fruit crops harvested and safely stored, winter is mainly a time for maintenance, pruning and taking precautions against pests and diseases. However, even now some fruits – such as strawberries and rhubarb – can be forced into life ready for an early harvest in spring.

Winter checklist

■ **Inspect stored** fruit every two to three weeks. Use any that is showing signs of deterioration, and discard rotting fruits.

■ **Continue planting** new fruit when conditions are suitable.

■ **Check ties** and supports: secure, adjust or repair.

■ **Clear weeds** for a distance of 60cm (2ft) around fruit plants and hoe the surface to expose pest eggs and larvae to foraging birds.

Prune apple trees while dormant to encourage new growth in spring.

■ **Prune gooseberries** and autumn-fruiting raspberries by cutting all canes down to 5–8cm (2–3in).

■ **Finish taking hardwood** cuttings of bush fruits while plants are dormant.

■ **Carry out essential** winter pruning before the end of January (see right).

■ **Look over** blackcurrant bushes for big bud (see below).

■ **Check grease** bands on fruit trees; reapply grease if needed.

■ **Deal with** canker on apple and pear trees (see opposite).

■ **Apply a winter** wash to dormant fruit trees (see opposite).

■ **Guard peaches** and nectarines from peach leaf curl with screens of polythene, and spray with copper-based fungicide.

■ **Sow grass seed** right up to the trunks of mature fruit trees if yields are low – the grass helps restore nutrients in the soil.

■ **Start fruits** under glass into growth.

■ **Place cloches** over strawberry plants to force early crops.

■ **Cover rhubarb** with boxes or forcing pots for an early harvest.

Winter pruning

A simple winter pruning routine applies to all tree and bush fruits, except plums, cherries, peaches and other stone fruits. These are pruned in spring.

■ **Cut back** dead, damaged or diseased stems.

■ **Remove branches** that cross or grow towards the centre; bushes should be kept open-centred in a goblet shape.

■ **Shorten those sideshoots** of cordons, espaliers and fans that were summer-pruned to four or five leaves; shorten to just one or two buds. For gooseberries and red and white currants, also prune back the tips of main branches.

■ **Thin out congested** spurs on mature trained forms of apple and pear; shorten long spurs by half.

■ **Encourage sideshoots** and spurs to develop on young espalier and fan-trained fruit by shortening main branches by half. Cut to a downward-facing bud.

■ **On overgrown or neglected** trees, cut out one or two main branches to admit more light and air and encourage new growth.

Treating pests and diseases

There are measures you can take now to protect plants from pests and diseases.

Blackcurrant big bud Blackcurrant gall mites overwinter inside buds, causing them to swell and fail to develop. The mites also spread reversion virus, an incurable disease. Check bushes in winter and early spring for the characteristic fat, rounded buds. Pick off any you find and destroy them.

Pruning gooseberries

1 Shorten to two buds all sideshoots that were summer-pruned to five leaves, and remove thin or spindly shoots.

2 Cut out one or two of the old, dark branches where young shoots are growing and tie these in as replacements.

3 Remove any surplus shoots growing from the base, clear weeds and mulch with straw, bracken or well-rotted manure.

Apple and pear canker This fungal disease can be serious if allowed to spread unchecked. Cracks and lesions develop on branches and at the base of spurs and sideshoots, causing them to die back if infection rings the stem. The disease is most prevalent on wet soils and is often controlled by improving drainage. Some apple varieties, such as 'Cox's Orange Pippin', are particularly vulnerable, whereas 'Bramley's Seedling', 'Lane's Prince Albert' and 'Newton Wonder' are more resistant.

■ **Remove diseased** and mummified fruits.
■ **Prune back** affected shoots and cut out lesions on main stems; paint the cuts with fungicidal wound paint.
■ **Sow grass or turf** round older trees to prevent rain splashes, which spread spores.
■ **Remove and destroy** badly infected trees.

Winter washing fruit Painting or spraying fruit trees with a tar-oil winter wash is a traditional way of killing overwintering pest larvae and eggs, disease spores, moss and lichen. This wash is toxic, so the area under the trees should be covered with plastic sheeting or thick layers of newspaper before treatment. The wash will kill the eggs and larvae of beneficial insects, as well as fruit pests.

Canker is a potentially serious fungal disease of apple and pear trees, most often caused by wet conditions.

A well-planned kitchen garden will continue to provide fresh vegetables for the table throughout winter. Late and hardy varieties survive the harshest frosts, while less hardy plants can be transferred to a greenhouse. Even the airing cupboard can be employed to produce 'chicons' from chicory roots.

Brussels sprout, late

Brassica oleracea Gemmifera Group

As mid-season varieties finish cropping in early winter, late varieties, such as 'Wellington' and 'Fortress', extend supplies until spring. Hardy.

Site Sun or light shade, sheltered. Deep, rich very firm soil, limed to pH7 or higher.

How to grow Sow in late April in a nursery bed outdoors and thin seedlings to 8cm (3in) apart. Transplant 60cm (2ft) apart when five to six weeks old. Water freely when dry and use a high-potash feed in midsummer. Stake on windy sites. Remove yellow leaves and net against birds. Pull up stems for stripping indoors. Harvest leafy tops to eat as greens.

Cabbage, winter

Brassica oleracea Capitata Group

Large plants with solid heads and a distinctive flavour. Many varieties have dark, crinkled leaves tinted blue or red. Hardy.

Site Sun. Rich firm soil, limed to pH7.

How to grow Sow in late April in a nursery bed outdoors and thin seedlings to 8cm (3in) apart. Transplant 50cm (20in) apart each way when six to eight weeks old. Water in dry weather and protect from birds. In exposed gardens earth up the stems in early winter for stability. Cut heads as required or pull up with the roots and suspend in a frost-free shed. Use by early spring.

Celeriac

Apium graveolens var. *rapaceum*

Rugged vegetable with celery-flavoured bulbous stem, great in winter stews. Hardy.

Site Sun or light shade. Rich moist soil.

How to grow Sow indoors in mid-spring and prick out seedlings individually into cell trays or small pots. Plant out 30cm (12in) apart when about 8cm (3in) tall. Water freely in dry weather and mulch. Pull off lower leaves and secondary growing tips every few weeks. Harvest from autumn and leave in the ground over winter.

Chicory, heading

Cichorium intybus

Crunchy salad crop with a slightly bitter flavour. The large green 'sugar loaf' type

and various red chicories, often called radicchio, are outdoor crops for autumn and early winter, or throughout winter if grown under cover. Not fully hardy.
Site Sun. Fertile and well-drained soil.
How to grow Sow in succession from April to July for harvesting from August to December. Plants can be sown *in situ* and thinned to 25–30cm (10–12in) apart each way; transplant midsummer thinnings to a coldframe or cool greenhouse for winter use. Water well in dry weather. Harvest complete heads as required.

Chicory, witloof

Cichorium intybus
Produces loose heads of leaves and thick roots that can be dug up and forced in an airing cupboard or cellar to produce fat buds called chicons. Surplus plants can be left to produce exquisite blue flowers the following year or moved to a wild garden. Hardy.
Site Sun. Fertile and well-drained soil.

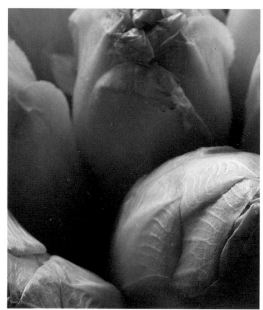

How to grow Sow outdoors in mid to late spring and thin seedlings to 23–25cm (9–10in) apart each way. Water well in dry weather. In early winter, dig up a few roots at a time, trim the thickest to 15cm (6in) and cut off the leaves about 2–3cm (1in) from

their base. Pack the roots upright in a box or pot of moist soil and put in a dark place until chicons appear. Cut when 10–15cm (4–6in) long; discard exhausted roots.

Horseradish

Armoracia rusticana
The hot, pungent flavour of this robust perennial's roots is in sauces and dips. Mild in spring but fiery in autumn. Hardy.
Site Sun or dappled shade. Light moist soil.
How to grow Sow or plant in spring. Control spread of older plants by chopping out wayward roots before they establish. To grow as an annual, plant root cuttings in spring for lifting in late autumn or winter.

Kale

Brassica oleracea Acephala Group
This annual or biennial leaf crop often supplies juicy 'greens' when other vegetables have succumbed in a hard winter. Different varieties have plain, sometimes red-tinted leaves or curly green or rich red foliage that is tightly crimped like parsley. Hardy.
Site Sun. Most even light soils with added compost or rotted manure.
How to grow Sow outdoors in May in a nursery bed and thin seedlings to 8cm (3in) apart. Transplant when about eight weeks old, 60cm (2ft) apart and keep well watered. Surplus kale can be transplanted to flower borders for winter bedding. Pick young leaves and whole shoots regularly from November until April.

Leek, late

Allium porrum
Versatile and richly flavoured undemanding crop that can withstand harsh weather. Winter leek varieties are bulkier than early ones, with thicker squat stems and dark, sometimes steely blue or purple-tinted foliage; 'Cortina', 'Apollo', 'Giant Winter' and 'Bleu de Solaise' are all good. Hardy.
Site Sun or light shade. Deep, rich soil with plenty of added compost.

How to grow Sow in late April and May in a nursery bed outdoors and thin seedlings to 4cm (1½in) apart. Plant out 20–23cm (8–9in) apart when 15–20cm (6–8in) tall, dropping into a 15cm (6in) deep hole made using a dibber. Water after planting and regularly throughout summer. Dig up as needed from early winter onwards; when hard frost is likely, lift several plants, trim leaves and roots and store in a cool, frost-free place, wrapped in newspaper.

Lettuce, winter

Lactuca sativa

Fresh lettuce can be available even in the depths of winter by using greenhouse varieties that are tolerant of short days and low light levels, such as 'Kellys', 'Novita' and 'Valdor'. In mild gardens these may be grown outdoors, preferably under cloches. Hardy.

Site Sun. Moist and well-drained soil.

How to grow Sow in September in modular trays indoors and transplant 20–25cm (8–10in) apart each way when 5–8cm (2–3in) high. Keep moist, but avoid overwatering. Ventilate freely if under glass except in frosty weather. Cut either complete heads or a few leaves from each young plant as loose-leaf lettuce.

Parsnip

Pastinaca sativa

Popular as a roast vegetable, parsnips are a reliable winter root that improves as the season progresses. Long varieties such as 'Tender and True' suit deep, light soils; for shallow soils, try a shorter kind like 'Avonresister'. Always use fresh seeds, as they do not keep well. Hardy.

Site Sun. Deeply dug soil that is not acid or recently manured.

How to grow Sow outdoors in March to May in rows 30cm (12in) apart and thin to 8–15cm (3–6in) apart, depending on the size of root required. Water regularly in dry weather to prevent splitting, and pull weeds by hand – hoeing can damage the tops. Start digging up roots in mid-autumn. To make lifting easier in a severe winter, cover rows with straw or leaves.

Radish, winter

Raphanus sativus

Although small summer radishes may still be available in a cold frame or greenhouse, the most reliable kinds for winter use are the large Spanish or Chinese varieties, like 'China Rose' or red-fleshed 'Manhangtong', and the long white Japanese mooli or daikon. Flavour and use are as for summer radishes. Not fully hardy.

Site Sun. Light soil.

How to grow Sow outdoors in August, in rows 25cm (10in) apart, and thin seedlings to about 15cm (6in) apart according to variety. Keep moist, but avoid over-watering. Crops are mature after about three months' growth and can be lifted as required.

Rhubarb, forced

Rheum x hybridum

Cover established crowns with cloches where they grow for early spring use, but can be forced in warmth and darkness for an even earlier harvest. Plants are useless after forcing, but divisions can be taken for replanting before forcing takes place. Hardy.
Site Dark frost-free place.

How to grow Dig up two to three-year-old crowns in November. Leave on the soil surface exposed to frost for two to three weeks then pack side by side in soil, old potting compost, straw or leaves and put in a dark place. Water well and do not allow to dry out. Ready to harvest after five to six weeks at 10ºC (50ºF).

Sage

Salvia officinalis

Aromatic shrubby evergreen with grey-green leaves used as a flavouring, especially for stuffing and meat dishes. Milder-flavoured, variegated and coloured kinds are good for shrub borders. Hardy.
Site Sun. Well-drained soil, not acid.

How to grow Prune hard to shape in spring and trim after flowering. Replace after four to five years. Sow under glass in March and plant out after the last frosts 45cm (18in) apart or take softwood cuttings in early summer. Protect in the first winter. Use soil-based or soil-less compost, both with added grit, for container-grown plants.

Spinach, winter

Spinacia oleracea

Fast-growing annual leaf vegetable. Varieties such as 'Bergola' and 'Sigmaleaf' are

available from December, but with cloche protection can be cropped throughout winter. In very cold gardens, perpetual spinach or spinach beet may be a more productive alternative. Hardy.
Site Sun. Fertile, well-drained soil.

How to grow Sow outdoors in August and September, in rows 30cm (12in) apart, and thin seedlings to clusters 15cm (6in) apart. Keep well watered at all times. Cover with cloches from late October. Harvest a few leaves from each plant.

Swede

Brassica napus var. *napobrassica*

This sweet, yellow-fleshed root needs a long growing season. Swedes can be overwintered in the ground, but keep their quality better if stored in boxes of sand. Ridging up surplus roots with soil in midwinter will produce young, semi-blanched 'spring greens'. Hardy.
Site Sun or light shade. Rich, moist soil, limed to pH7.

How to grow Sow outdoors in June for winter use and in April for autumn use. Space rows 40cm (16in) apart and thin seedlings to 25cm (10in) apart. Water regularly in dry weather. Dig roots as required; lift for storing in early winter.

© RD = Reader's Digest Association, All artwork=© Reader's Digest Association
T=Top, **B**=Bottom, **L**=Left, **R**=Right, **C**=Centre

Cover DigitalVision/Martin Poole **1** iStockphoto.com/Pierre-Gilles Markioli **2–3** ShutterStock, Inc/Julie DeGuia **4 L** iStockphoto.com/Eric Naud **R** iStockphoto.com/Ron Hohenhaus **5 TL** iStockphoto.com/Johnny Scriv **R** ShutterStock, Inc/Kati Molin **6** ShutterStock, Inc/Nicholas Sutcliffe **8–9** ShutterStock, Inc/Mishella **10** © RD/Mark Winwood **11** © RD/Maddie Thornhill **12** © RD/Mark Winwood **13** iStockphoto.com/ Brett Charlton **14** © RD/Sarah Cuttle **15 TL** © RD/Maddie Thornhill **BR** © RD/Mark Winwood **16** © RD/Mike Newton **17 T** Garden World Images/R Loader **B** Gap Photos Ltd/Mark Bolton **18** Garden World Images/C Jenkins **19** © RD/Debbie Patterson **20** © RD/Debbie Patterson **21** © RD/Mark Winwood **22** © RD/Sarah Cuttle **23 L** Garden World Images/R Loader **R** © RD/Mark Winwood **24 T** Gap Photos Ltd/Friedrich Strauss **BR** Maddie Thornhill **25** © RD/Sarah Cuttle **T** Garden World Images/Geoff Kidd **26** Garden World Images/Maddie Thornhill **27** © RD/Mark Winwood **28 T** Maddie Thornhill **B** Garden World Images/R Coates **29 L** Maddie Thornhill **R** Gap Photos Ltd/Juliette Wade **30 T** Gap Photos Ltd/Howard Rice **B** © RD/Maddie Thornhill **31 L** Mike Newton **R** Gap Photos Ltd/Rob Whitworth **32 L** Gap Photos Ltd/ J S Sira **R** Gap Photos Ltd/Jonathan Buckley **33 L** © Reader'sDigest/Maddie Thornhill **R** Garden World Images/Dave Bevan **34 TR** Garden World Images/John Swithinbank **BL, BR** © RD/Maddie Thornhill **35 L** © RD/Maddie Thornhill **R** Gap Photos Ltd/Fredrich Strauss **36** Gap Photos Ltd/Mark Bolton **L** Garden World Images/T Sims **37 TL** Garden World Images/R Coates **BL** © RD/Maddie Thornhill **BR** Mike Newton **38–39** iStockphoto.com/Ron Hohenhaus **40** iStockphoto.com/Vera Bogaerts **41** © RD/Mark Winwood **43 T** ShutterStock, Inc/R Gino Santa Maria **B** © RD/Maddie Thornhill **44 T** © RD/Mark Winwood **B** © RD/Maddie Thornhill **45** Gap Photos Ltd/Michael Howes **46** ShutterStock, Inc/Anne Kitzman **47** © RD/Mark Winwood **48** Gap Photos Ltd/Maddie Thornhill **49 T** © RD/Mark Winwood **B** Photolibrary Group/Robert Golden **50** ShutterStock, Inc/Spauln **52** Mike Newton **53** © RD/Mark Winwood **54 T** Mike Newton **B** ShutterStock, Inc/Kristy Batie **55 TL, B** © RD/Sarah Cuttle **TR** © RD/Mark Winwood **56** © RD/Sarah Cuttle **57** Photolibrary Group/Ron Sutherland **58** Andrew Lawson **60** © RD/Sarah Cuttle **61** © RD/Mark Winwood **63** ShutterStock, Inc/Olga Utlyakova **64 TR, BL** © RD/Mark Winwood **BR** Gap Photos Ltd/ S & O Mathews **65** Garden World Images **66 TL** © RD/Maddie Thornhill **TR, BR** © RD/Mark Winwood **67** Gap Photos Ltd/Howard Rice **68 T** © RD/Sarah Cuttle **BL** © RD/Maddie Thornhill **69** iStockphoto.com/Kathy Puckett **70** © RD/Mark Winwood **71 L** iStockphoto.com/Viorika Prikhodko **R** © RD/Maddie Thornhill **72** © RD/Mark Bolton **73** © RD/Maddie Thornhill **74** © RD/Sarah Cuttle **75** The Garden Collection/Derek St Romaine **76** Gap Photos Ltd/Paul Debois **77** © RD/Maddie Thornhill **78–79** © RD **80 CR** © RD **BL** © RD/Maddie Thornhill **81** Gap Photos Ltd/Clive Nichols **82–83** ShutterStock, Inc/Craig Barhorst **84** iStockphoto.com/Kaaja **85 TL** © RD/Mike Newton **B** © RD/Mark Winwood **86** iStockphoto.com/Loretta Hostettler **87** © RD/Mark Winwood **88** © RD/Mike Newton **89** Gap Photos Ltd/Howard Rice **90** Garden World Images/J Thompson **91** iStockphoto.com/AtWaG **92** Garden World Images/D Bevan **93** © RD/Mark Winwood **94** Photolibrary Group/Georgia Glynn-Smith **95 T** Garden World Images/F Emonds **B** © RD/Mark Winwood **96 B** © RD/Debbie Patterson **98 TL** © RD/Sarah Cuttle **B** © RD/Mark Winwood **99** © RD/Sarah Cuttle **100** © RD/Maddie Thornhill **101 L** © RD/Maddie Thornhill **R** Garden World Images/John Swithinbank **102–103** © RD/Maddie Thornhill **104–105** ShutterStock, Inc/Sally Wallis **106** © RD/Maddie Thornhill **107** © RD/Mark Winwood **108 TR** © RD/Sarah Cuttle **CL, BR** © RD/Mark Winwood **109** © RD/Maddie Thornhill **110** © RD/Sarah Cuttle **111** © RD/Mark Winwood **113 T** © RD/Sarah Cuttle **B** Photolibrary Group/M Howes **114** © RD/Mike Newton **115** Photolibrary Group/Mark Bolton **116 L** © RD/Mark Winwood **R** © RD/Sarah Cuttle **117 T** Photolibrary Group/C Boursnell **B** © RD/Mark Winwood **118–119** © RD/Mark Winwood **120 T** © RD/Maddie Thornhill **B** ShutterStock, Inc/Dwight Smith **121–123** © RD/Maddie Thornhill

Reader's Digest Year-round Kitchen Garden is based on material in *The Complete Guide to Gardening Season by Season*, published by The Reader's Digest Association Limited, London.

First Edition Copyright © 2008

The Reader's Digest Association Limited, 11 Westferry Circus, Canary Wharf, London E14 4HE **www.readersdigest.co.uk**

Editors Caroline Smith, Diane Cross
Art Editors Kate Harris, Conorde Clarke
Proofreader Rosemary Wighton
Indexer Marie Lorimer
Picture Researcher Rosie Taylor

Reader's Digest General Books
Editorial Director Julian Browne
Art Director Anne-Marie Bulat
Managing Editor Nina Hathway
Head of Book Development Sarah Bloxham
Picture Resource Manager Sarah Stewart-Richardson
Pre-press Account Manager Dean Russell
Production Controller Sandra Fuller
Product Production Manager Claudette Bramble

Origination Colour Systems Limited, London
Printed in China

We are committed both to the quality of our products and the service we provide to our customers. We value your comments, so please do contact us on **08705 113366** or via our website at **www.readersdigest.co.uk**

If you have any comments or suggestions about the content of our books, email us at **gbeditorial@readersdigest.co.uk**

ISBN 978 0 276 44387 9
BOOK CODE 400-383 UP0000-1
ORACLE CODE 250012536H.00.24